The Magic Gaze: Decoding Thoughts through Eyes and Gestures

Authored By

Yuvika Singh
The ICFAI University
Himachal Pradesh
India

The Magic Gaze: Decoding Thoughts through Eyes and Gestures

Author: Yuvika Singh

ISBN (Online): 979-8-89881-015-3

ISBN (Print): 979-8-89881-016-0

ISBN (Paperback): 979-8-89881-017-7

Published by Bentham Science Publishers Pte. Ltd. Singapore, in collaboration with Eureka Conferences, USA. All Rights Reserved.

First published in 2025.

need for a court order if at any point you breach any terms of this License Agreement. In no event will any delay or failure by Bentham Science Publishers in enforcing your compliance with this License Agreement constitute a waiver of any of its rights.

3. You acknowledge that you have read this License Agreement, and agree to be bound by its terms and conditions. To the extent that any other terms and conditions presented on any website of Bentham Science Publishers conflict with, or are inconsistent with, the terms and conditions set out in this License Agreement, you acknowledge that the terms and conditions set out in this License Agreement shall prevail.

Bentham Science Publishers Pte. Ltd.
No. 9 Raffles Place
Office No. 26-01
Singapore 048619
Singapore
Email: subscriptions@benthamscience.net

CONTENTS

FOREWORD

Nonverbal communication, the often overlooked yet profoundly influential aspect of human interaction, serves as the cornerstone of this compelling exploration into the language beyond words. *The Magic Gaze: Decoding Thoughts through Eyes and Gestures* was conceived to illuminate how the subtleties of gestures, facial expressions, eye movements, and posture can convey meaning as powerfully, if not more so, than spoken language.

Our motivation as editors in supporting this work stemmed from the increasing relevance of nonverbal cues in a world where digital interactions and diverse cultures intersect daily. While traditional communication studies focus extensively on verbal exchanges, there remains a critical need to decode the rich tapestry of signals humans use subconsciously. This book serves as a comprehensive guide, unraveling the complex symphony of silent communication through meticulously researched chapters that blend academic rigor with practical applications.

The author's dedication to detailing this field is evident in the way each chapter builds a deeper understanding, from the foundational principles of body language to the intricate nuances of micro-expressions and cultural differences. The text also embraces modern scientific advancements, exploring how technologies like pupillometry reveal the unspoken truths about cognition and emotion. Furthermore, practical strategies for sharpening observation skills make this book an invaluable resource for professionals in psychology, education, law enforcement, and anyone eager to enhance their interpersonal awareness.

As an editor of the book, it is my hope that *The Magic Gaze: Decoding Thoughts through Eyes and Gestures* becomes a tool for readers to gain not only insight into the behaviors of others but also a greater awareness of their own unspoken messages. As you turn the pages, we invite you to discover the intricate world of nonverbal communication—a domain where silence speaks volumes and understanding deepens connection.

Rania Lampou
Global Educator and STEM Instructor
Directorate of Educational Technology and Innovation
Greek Ministry of Education
Religious Affairs and Sports
Marousi, Greece

PREFACE

In the dynamic flow of human interaction, much of our communication occurs beyond spoken words. The eyes, posture, hand movements, and even the dilation of pupils—these unspoken cues often carry a wealth of meaning, sometimes more powerful than words themselves. *The Magic Gaze: Decoding Thoughts through Eyes and Gestures* invites you to delve into this fascinating realm of nonverbal communication, offering insights that will transform the way you perceive and interact with the world.

This book was born out of a deep passion for understanding the silent language that shapes our interactions. You will discover how eye movements, micro-expressions, and body language work in concert to convey emotions, intentions, and even unconscious thoughts. The role of cultural context in shaping nonverbal signals is another central theme, allowing you to develop a nuanced appreciation of global communication practices. We also take a close look into the psychology behind facial expressions and the profound insights offered by pupillometry, revealing how subtle shifts in our bodies can provide powerful windows into our emotions and cognitive processes.

Chapters on deception detection and honing observational skills offer practical techniques that empower you to interpret unspoken messages. As we approach the book's conclusion, we explore the expanding frontiers of human perception—intuition and beyond-sense awareness—challenging readers to think beyond the five senses and consider the untapped potential of human perception.

I extend my heartfelt gratitude to Professor Rania Lampou, whose insightful editorial guidance has been instrumental in shaping this book. Her expertise has enriched this work in ways that enhance its depth and accessibility.

The Magic Gaze is designed not only as a resource for professionals in fields such as psychology, medicine, law enforcement, business, and education but also for anyone eager to enhance their interpersonal communication and deepen their understanding of human behavior. By mastering the art of interpreting nonverbal cues, you will not only improve your ability to connect with others but also unlock profound insights into their thoughts and emotions. As the author of this book, I trust it will inspire you to forge deeper, more intuitive connections with the world around you.

Yuvika Singh
The ICFAI University
Himachal Pradesh, India

CHAPTER 1

The Science of Nonverbal Communication

Abstract: Nonverbal communication is a complex system of signals that includes facial expressions, gestures, posture, and spatial behavior, all essential for human interaction. This chapter explores the science behind nonverbal communication, focusing on its biological and cultural origins, and emphasizes how nonverbal cues enhance or contradict verbal messages. Exploring psychological and neurological aspects, the chapter focuses on empathy, emotional recognition, and how nonverbal cues influence judgments of trustworthiness and leadership, influencing decision-making processes. Real-life examples illustrate the critical role of nonverbal cues across contexts, from professional interactions to personal relationships. This chapter offers insights into interpreting these cues to improve both personal and professional relationships.

Keywords: Facial expressions, Gestures, Human interaction, Nonverbal communication, Spatial behavior.

INTRODUCTION

Nonverbal communication is a crucial aspect of human interaction, encompassing all forms of communication that do not rely on spoken or written language. This includes a wide range of behaviors such as facial expressions, body language, gestures, eye contact, touch, and the use of space and time. These nonverbal cues often carry more weight than verbal communication, as they can reveal underlying emotions, attitudes, and intentions that words alone may fail to convey.

Importance of Nonverbal Communication

The significance of nonverbal communication in human interaction is profound. Research indicates that a substantial portion of communication effectiveness is derived from nonverbal cues. Mehrabian (1971) proposed a widely cited breakdown of emotional communications: 55% attributed to facial expressions and body language, 38% to tone of voice, and only 7% to actual words. However, this study was conducted in a highly specific context, focusing on ambiguous or emotionally charged messages, and has been frequently misinterpreted. Although Mehrabian's 7-38-55 rule is based on a limited study, the mere fact that it is so commonly cited, even overused, highlights the important role people assign to nonverbal signals in human communication, especially in contexts where emotions and interpersonal dynamics are involved. Recognizing both the influence and limitations of this rule ensures a more nuanced understanding of nonverbal communication (Amsel, 2019). Nonverbal communication aids in building trust, expressing empathy, and navigating social interactions. It allows individuals to convey sincerity, attentiveness, and understanding, which are essential for effective communication in both personal and professional settings. For example, consistent eye contact can signal confidence and attentiveness, while open body language can indicate approachability and openness to dialogue. Conversely, crossed arms or avoiding eye contact may be interpreted as defensiveness or disinterest. Given its vital role in human interaction, nonverbal communication has been studied for centuries, with early explorations setting the foundation for modern research.

Historical Context and Development

The study of nonverbal communication has deep historical roots, with early explorations of the topic dating back to the 19th century. Charles Darwin's 1872 book, *The Expression of the Emotions in Man and Animals*, is often cited as one of the foundational works in the field. Darwin's work laid the groundwork for understanding how nonverbal behaviors, particularly facial expressions, are universal across cultures and play a key role in conveying emotions (Darwin, 1872). However, it was not until the mid-20th century that systematic research on nonverbal communication began to emerge as a distinct field of study. Pioneers such as Ray Birdwhistell and Edward T. Hall were instrumental in advancing the understanding of nonverbal behavior. Birdwhistell, often regarded as the founder of kinesics (the study of body motion communication), introduced the idea that body language is a structured system of communication, much like spoken language. In his 1952 book *Introduction to Kinesics*, Birdwhistell argued that movements and gestures could be analyzed and interpreted systematically.

Edward T. Hall, on the other hand, focused on the concept of proxemics, which examines the use of space in communication. Hall's work in the 1960s, particularly his book *The Hidden Dimension* (1966), introduced the idea that the physical distance between people during interactions is culturally dependent and can convey a range of social signals, from intimacy to power dynamics. Building on these foundational studies, contemporary research has continued to explore and expand our understanding of nonverbal communication in diverse fields and contexts.

Contemporary Research and Applications

In contemporary research, nonverbal communication continues to be a vital area of study, with applications across various fields such as psychology, sociology, anthropology, and communication studies. Advances in technology, including neuroimaging and motion capture, have allowed researchers to explore nonverbal communication with greater precision, leading to new insights into how these cues influence human behavior. For instance, studies in social psychology have explored how nonverbal cues like facial expressions and body posture influence perceptions of leadership and competence (Darwin, 1872). In the field of medicine, nonverbal communication is recognized as a key component of doctor-patient interactions, where empathy and trust are crucial for effective care.

Moreover, nonverbal communication is increasingly relevant in a globalized world, where understanding cultural differences in nonverbal behavior is essential for successful cross-cultural communication. Scholars such as Paul Ekman have expanded upon Darwin's work, demonstrating that while certain facial expressions are universally recognized, the way they are interpreted and expressed can vary significantly across cultures (Ekman, 1993).

The Biological Basis of Nonverbal Communication

Nonverbal communication, with its deep roots in human evolution and biology, is integral to how we interact and connect with one another. This form of communication, which predates the development of verbal language, has been essential for survival, social bonding, and the coordination of group activities among early human ancestors. The biological underpinnings of nonverbal communication can be traced to specific neural structures and processes that have evolved to facilitate the recognition, interpretation, and generation of nonverbal signals (Ambady & Weisbuch, 2010).

Evolutionary Perspective

From an evolutionary standpoint, nonverbal communication likely emerged as one of the earliest forms of interaction among our ancestors. Long before the development of complex spoken languages, early humans relied on facial expressions, gestures, and vocalizations to convey important information. These nonverbal cues were crucial for survival, as they allowed individuals to warn others of potential dangers, express emotions such as fear or aggression, and coordinate activities like hunting or defending territory (Darwin, 1872).

Research in evolutionary biology suggests that the ability to communicate nonverbally provides a significant adaptive advantage. For example, facial expressions of emotion are believed to have evolved as universal signals that can be easily recognized across different human cultures. This universality supports the idea that such expressions serve fundamental social and survival functions. Six basic emotions—happiness, sadness, fear, anger, surprise, and disgust—that are universally recognized through facial expressions provide evidence for the evolutionary basis of these nonverbal cues (Ekman, 1993).

Neurological Basis

Nonverbal communication is deeply embedded in the brain's structure, with several key regions involved in the processing and generation of nonverbal cues. The limbic system, often referred to as the "emotional brain," plays a central role in this process. The amygdala, a critical component of the limbic system, is particularly involved in processing emotional stimuli, especially those related to fear and threat. Studies have shown that the amygdala is activated when individuals view faces expressing fear, highlighting its role in detecting potential dangers in the environment (Adolphs, 2002). Another important brain structure involved in nonverbal communication is the prefrontal cortex, which is responsible for higher-order cognitive functions such as decision-making and social behavior. The prefrontal cortex helps integrate nonverbal cues with contextual information, enabling individuals to interpret the meaning of these cues in a given social situation.

Mirror Neurons and Empathy

The discovery of mirror neurons has further illuminated the neurological basis of nonverbal communication. Mirror neurons are a type of brain cell that responds both when an individual performs an action and when they observe someone else performing the same action. First identified in the premotor cortex of macaque monkeys, these neurons have since been found in humans and are believed to play a key role in understanding and empathizing with others (Moskowitz, 2024; Rout, 2023;Rizzolatti & Craighero, 2004).

As shown in Fig. (**1**), mirror neurons are thought to be involved in the process of "mind reading," or the ability to infer the intentions and emotions of others based on their nonverbal behaviors. When we observe someone smiling, for example, mirror neurons in our brain may activate in a way that simulates the act of smiling, allowing us to understand the positive emotion being expressed. This mirroring mechanism is believed to underline empathy, as it enables us to "feel" what others are experiencing by internally replicating their emotional states.

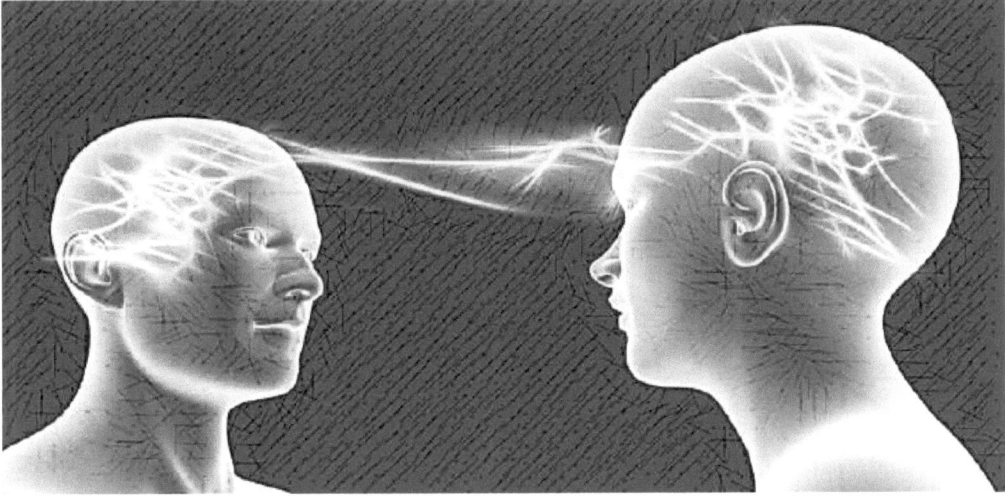

Fig. (1). Mirror neurons- human see, human do'. Source: Adapted from Moskowitz (2024); Rout (2023).

Research has also linked mirror neurons to the ability to understand and replicate gestures and facial expressions, which are crucial components of nonverbal communication. The activation of mirror neurons during the observation of nonverbal cues suggests that these neurons may facilitate social learning and the transmission of cultural norms and behaviors through imitation (Moskowitz, 2024).

TYPES OF NONVERBAL COMMUNICATION

Nonverbal communication is a multifaceted form of expression that encompasses a wide range of behaviors and signals, as shown in Fig. (**2**), beyond spoken language. These signals can convey emotions, attitudes, and intentions, often more effectively than words. Understanding the different types of nonverbal communication is crucial for interpreting human interactions accurately (Noroozi *et al.*, 2021).

Below, the key types of nonverbal communication are elaborated upon with examples and cultural considerations (Noroozi *et al.*, 2021).

Fig. (2). Non-verbal communication.
Source: Adapted from Birdwhistell (1970); Ekman & Friesen (1971); Noroozi *et al.* (2021).

Kinesics: Body Movements

Kinesics refers to the study of body movements, including gestures, postures, and facial expressions, which are among the most visible and immediate forms of nonverbal communication (Birdwhistell, 1970):

Gestures

Gestures are deliberate movements of the hands, arms, or body that convey specific messages. For example, a thumbs-up gesture is commonly understood as a sign of approval or agreement in many Western cultures. However, gestures can have different meanings across cultures; for instance, the "OK" hand gesture (forming a circle with the thumb and forefinger) is positive in the United States but can be offensive in some other countries like Brazil.

Posture

Posture refers to the way individuals hold their body when standing, sitting, or moving. It can indicate a person's confidence, openness, or defensiveness. For example, standing straight with shoulders back is often associated with confidence, while slouching may suggest a lack of energy or interest.

Facial Expressions

Facial expressions are powerful indicators of emotions. A smile typically conveys happiness or friendliness, while a frown can indicate displeasure or confusion. Research by Paul Ekman has shown that certain facial expressions, such as those for happiness, sadness, fear, and anger, are universally recognized across different cultures, suggesting an evolutionary basis for these expressions (Ekman & Friesen, 1971).

While body movements like gestures and facial expressions are key to conveying emotions, the physical space we maintain during interactions—studied in proxemics—also plays a critical role in shaping communication.

Proxemics: Use of Personal Space

Proxemics, a concept introduced by anthropologist Edward T. Hall, involves the study of how people use and perceive the physical space around them. The use of personal space can vary greatly depending on cultural norms, the nature of the relationship, and the context of the interaction (Gunawan, 2021):

Intimate Distance (0-18 inches):

This zone is reserved for close personal relationships, such as those between family members, romantic partners, or very close friends. At this distance, individuals can engage in intimate touch and quiet conversation.

Personal Distance (18 inches - 4 feet):

This space is typically used for interactions with friends and acquaintances. It allows for personal conversation while maintaining a comfortable distance.

Social Distance (4-12 feet):

Social distance is common in interactions with strangers and colleagues or during formal settings. It is the distance typically maintained in professional or casual social gatherings.

Public Distance (more than 12 feet):

Public distance is used for public speaking or when addressing a large group. At this distance, communication tends to be more formal, and nonverbal cues such as gestures and vocal volume become more exaggerated.

Fig. (**3**) reveals the ***Hall's Proxemics Zone***. The appropriate use of these distance zones can vary significantly across cultures. For example, people from Mediterranean and Latin American cultures often prefer closer personal distances, while individuals from Northern European and East Asian cultures may prefer more personal space during interactions (Gunawan, 2021; Hall, 1966). While proxemics highlights the significance of personal space in communication, another vital form of nonverbal interaction is haptics, which explores the power of touch in conveying emotions and intentions.

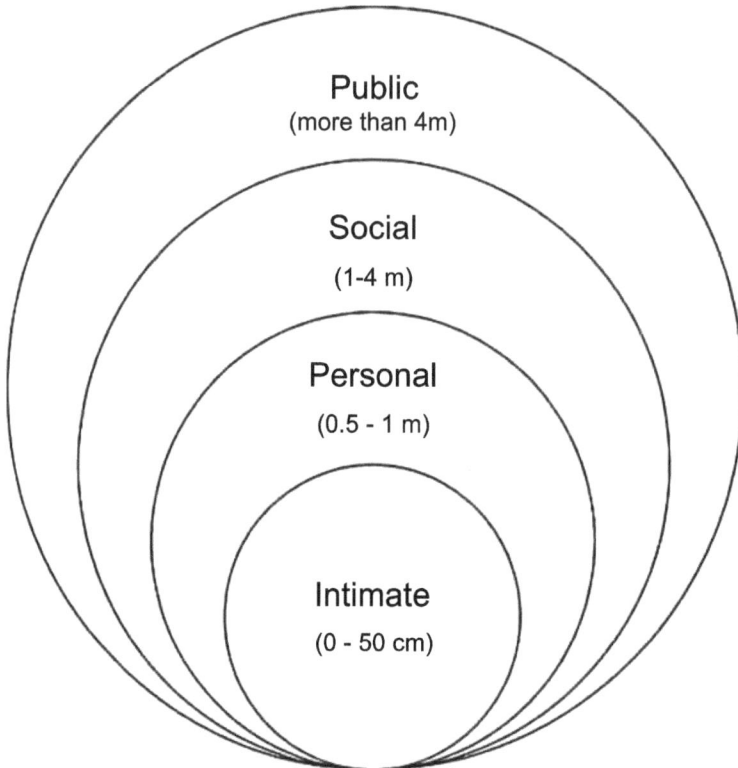

Fig. (3). Non-verbal communication. Source: Adapted from Gunawan (2021); Hall (1966).

Haptics: Communication Through Touch

Haptics is the study of touch as a form of nonverbal communication. Touch is a powerful way to convey emotions and messages, but its meaning can vary widely depending on the context, the relationship between the individuals, and cultural norms (Goman, 2011; Jourard, 1966):

Handshakes

A handshake is a common form of greeting in many cultures, conveying professionalism, respect, or agreement. The firmness of the handshake can also carry meaning, with a firm handshake often interpreted as a sign of confidence.

Pats and Hugs

A pat on the back can be a sign of encouragement or congratulations, while a hug typically conveys warmth, affection, or comfort. However, the acceptability of these touches depends on the cultural context; for example, in some cultures, hugging is a common greeting, while in others, it may be reserved for close relationships only.

Cultural Variations

The interpretation of touch varies significantly across cultures. For instance, in some Asian cultures, touch between individuals who are not close family members may be less common, while in Mediterranean cultures, more physical contact is the norm in social interactions. In business negotiations, Mediterranean cultures might favor closer proximity to establish rapport, while Northern European professionals may prefer maintaining a greater distance to ensure a sense of personal space and professionalism.

For leaders in a professional setting, understanding the appropriate use of touch—such as a handshake or a pat on the back—can enhance their connection with colleagues or subordinates, fostering a sense of trust and camaraderie.

Oculesics: Eye Behavior

Oculesics refers to the study of eye-related behaviors, including eye contact, gaze direction, and pupil dilation. The eyes are often referred to as the "windows to the soul," as they can reveal a great deal about a person's emotions and intentions (Argyle & Dean, 1965; Hess, 1975):

Eye Contact

Eye contact is one of the most direct forms of nonverbal communication. Sustained eye contact can indicate attention, interest, or dominance, while avoiding eye contact may suggest shyness, disinterest, or even deception. However, the cultural interpretation of eye contact varies; in some cultures, direct eye contact is considered a sign of respect and confidence, while in others, it may be seen as confrontational or disrespectful.

Gaze Direction

The direction of a person's gaze can signal where their attention is focused. For example, looking away while speaking might indicate distraction or discomfort, while maintaining a steady gaze can show interest and engagement.

Pupil Dilation

Pupil dilation can be an involuntary response to emotional stimuli. For instance, pupils may dilate when a person is experiencing strong emotions such as attraction or fear. Although subtle, this physiological response can convey significant information about a person's emotional state.

UNDERSTANDING THE INTERPLAY BETWEEN VERBAL AND NONVERBAL COMMUNICATION

The interplay between verbal and nonverbal communication is a complex and essential aspect of human interaction, a subject that has been thoroughly examined in academic research across fields like psychology, communication studies, and anthropology. Studies demonstrate that both forms of communication work in concert to convey meaning, with nonverbal cues often providing context, emphasis, and emotional depth to the spoken words. Grounded in seminal works by researchers such as Albert Mehrabian and Edward T. Hall, who analyzed the impact of facial expressions, gestures, and personal space, this section explores how verbal and nonverbal cues interact to create a fuller understanding of communication.

In particular, academic literature underscores the significance of nonverbal communication in high-stakes contexts, such as negotiations, conflicts, and other situations where stakes are high and interpretations of meaning become crucial. In these settings, nonverbal cues like body language, tone, and facial expressions can alter or reinforce the meanings conveyed through words, impacting trust, credibility, and emotional impact. Understanding this dynamic interaction enhances our ability to interpret messages accurately and respond effectively, enabling clearer, more meaningful communication and reducing potential misunderstandings. By examining the mechanisms through which verbal and nonverbal elements complement, contradict, substitute, regulate, and accentuate one another, this analysis provides a scholarly foundation for appreciating the multi-layered nature of human communication (Noroozi *et al.*, 2021; Zuckerman & Driver, 1985) (Fig. **4**).

Let's explore the key ways in which these two forms of communication interact:

Fig. (4). Non-verbal cues. Source: Adapted from Argyle (1988). Burgoon *et al.* (2016); Duncan (1972); Dutta (2024); Ekman (2003); Ekman & Friesen (1969). Knapp *et al.*, (2013); Mehrabian (1972); Noroozi *et al.*, (2021); Zuckerman & Driver, (1985).

Complementing

Nonverbal communication often serves to complement verbal messages, adding clarity and reinforcing the spoken words. When nonverbal cues align with what is being said, they strengthen the overall message, making it more convincing and impactful. For instance, in a negotiation, a statement like "We can reach an agreement" delivered with an open posture, a slight forward lean, and a calm tone conveys sincerity and willingness to cooperate, enhancing trust and credibility. Complementary nonverbal cues help ensure that the listener receives the intended message. This alignment between verbal and nonverbal communication builds trust and facilitates clear understanding, as the listener can rely on multiple channels of information to interpret the speaker's emotions and intentions (Burgoon *et al.*, 2016).

Contradicting

There are instances where nonverbal cues contradict verbal messages, creating confusion and often leading the listener to question the speaker's true feelings or intentions. In high-stress contexts, such as conflict resolution, saying, "I'm open to your ideas" while maintaining a rigid posture and crossed arms can signal defensiveness rather than openness. Contradictory signals are often interpreted as signs of deception, internal conflict, or emotional distress. When nonverbal communication contradicts verbal communication, it can undermine the speaker's credibility and make it difficult for the listener to trust the message. In such cases, nonverbal cues tend to carry more weight in the interpretation of the message (Mehrabian, 1972; Zuckerman & Driver, 1985).

Thus, the interplay between verbal and nonverbal communication is multifaceted, with each component adding layers of meaning that enhance or alter the interpretation of messages. In both casual and high-stakes interactions, understanding these dynamics can significantly improve clarity, trust, and rapport.

Substituting

Nonverbal communication can sometimes substitute for verbal communication entirely. In situations where words are unnecessary or inappropriate, nonverbal cues can convey the intended message effectively. Imagine in a high-stakes meeting, a simple nod might substitute a verbal "yes" in agreement to avoid interrupting the flow or maintain discretion. Similarly, a shrug of the shoulders can communicate uncertainty or indifference, effectively replacing the need to verbally say, "I don't know." Nonverbal substitutions are particularly valuable in cross-cultural communication, where language barriers might exist, and in situations requiring brevity or discretion (Knapp *et al.*, 2013).

Regulating

Nonverbal communication plays a crucial role in regulating the flow of conversation. Regulating, in communication, refers to the use of cues to manage and control the flow and pace of a conversation. Through gestures, facial expressions, and other nonverbal behaviors, individuals can signal when it is their turn to speak, when they are listening, or when they wish to interrupt or conclude a conversation. During a conversation, a listener might nod their head, maintain eye contact, and lean slightly forward to show they are engaged and encourage the speaker to continue. Conversely, looking away, checking a watch, or leaning back might signal that the listener is disinterested or that the conversation should wrap up. In high-stakes discussions, such as debates, nodding and maintaining eye contact can keep the speaker encouraged to continue while glancing away may subtly signal the desire to respond. Regulation through nonverbal cues helps ensure smooth and orderly communication. It allows participants in a conversation to manage turn-taking, avoid interruptions, and maintain the flow of dialogue. Effective regulation through nonverbal communication enhances mutual understanding and prevents misunderstandings (Duncan, 1972).

Accenting

Nonverbal communication can also accent or emphasize specific parts of a verbal message, adding intensity or focus to what is being said. Accenting in communication involves using nonverbal cues to add emphasis, intensity, or focus to specific parts of a verbal message. Through variations in tone, volume, facial expressions, or gestures, a speaker can highlight the most important parts of their message. A speaker might raise their voice or use hand gestures to emphasize key points during a speech, drawing the audience's attention to the most critical information. A sudden increase in volume or a pointed gesture can signal that a particular word or phrase is especially significant. In a persuasive speech or presentation, raising one's voice, pausing deliberately, or using emphatic hand gestures can draw attention to critical points, ensuring they resonate more with the audience. Accenting helps to convey the emotional intensity or importance of a message, guiding the listener to the core elements of what is being communicated. This technique enhances the effectiveness of the message and ensures that the key points are understood and remembered (Ekman, 2003).

Another significant aspect of nonverbal communication is the importance of alignment between verbal and nonverbal cues. When nonverbal behavior aligns with spoken words, it fosters trust and enhances the clarity of communication. In contrast, misalignment can lead to misunderstandings and misinterpretations, impacting the overall effectiveness of the interaction.

Alignment

When verbal and nonverbal communication align, they generally indicate congruence and authenticity. Such alignment suggests that the speaker is being honest and transparent, as both their words and nonverbal cues convey the same message. This consistency builds trust and facilitates clear and effective communication (Argyle,1988). In a supportive conversation, a person saying "I'm here for you" while gently touching the listener's hand and maintaining warm eye contact conveys genuine care and concern. The alignment between the verbal and nonverbal cues reassures the listener of the speaker's sincerity.

Misalignment between verbal and nonverbal communication can signal potential deception, internal conflict, or discomfort. When words and body language don't match, the listener may perceive the speaker as untrustworthy, confused, or insincere (Ekman & Friesen, 1969). A person expressing enthusiasm about a project but doing so with a flat tone of voice and a lack of facial expression may lead others to doubt their true level of interest. The discrepancy between the verbal and nonverbal cues creates ambiguity and can lead to misunderstandings.

Unconscious *vs.* Conscious Nonverbal Signals

Nonverbal communication represents a vital aspect of human interaction, encompassing a spectrum of behaviors that operate both unconsciously and consciously. These signals, often subtle yet powerful, provide insight into the emotions, intentions, and thoughts that may not always be conveyed through words alone. The complexity of nonverbal communication lies in the interplay between those behaviors that we unconsciously exhibit and those we consciously control. Understanding this distinction is essential for a nuanced interpretation of human behavior (Zuckerman & Driver, 1985).

Unconscious Nonverbal Signals

Many of the nonverbal cues we display occur without conscious thought, reflecting deep-seated emotional states and automatic responses that have been honed through evolution. These signals are often the most revealing, providing a window into the true feelings of an individual, even when their verbal communication may suggest otherwise. One of the most compelling examples of unconscious nonverbal behavior is micro-expression. These brief, involuntary facial expressions last only a fraction of a second, yet they can reveal genuine emotions that a person might be trying to conceal. For instance, a fleeting look of fear or anger may pass across someone's face before they can mask it with a smile. The study of micro-expressions, first brought to prominence by Paul Ekman and Wallace Friesen in 1969, has shown that these tiny facial movements are universal, transcending cultural boundaries and offering a glimpse into the innate aspects of our emotional responses. In addition to micro-expressions, other forms of unconscious nonverbal communication include automatic gestures and postures. For example, a person might cross their arms during a conversation, an action that might unconsciously signal defensiveness or discomfort. Such gestures are often made without deliberate intent, yet they communicate volumes about a person's internal state. Allan and Barbara (2004) discuss how body language, including these subtle gestures and postures, often operates on an unconscious level, providing critical insights into underlying emotions and attitudes (Dutta, 2024).

Conscious Nonverbal Signals

While much nonverbal communication happens unconsciously, individuals also engage in a range of behaviors that are more deliberate and controlled. These conscious nonverbal signals are often employed to complement or emphasize verbal communication, serving as tools to enhance the clarity and impact of the spoken word. Gestures are a prime example of conscious nonverbal behavior. A speaker might nod to indicate agreement or use hand movements to emphasize a point. These gestures are typically performed with awareness and intent, designed to reinforce the verbal message. However, even these consciously controlled behaviors can inadvertently reveal underlying emotions, particularly in moments of stress or distraction. As discussed by Knapp *et al.* (2013), while individuals consciously use gestures to complement their verbal communication, these actions can still provide unintentional cues about their true feelings. Posture, too, can be consciously managed to project a desired image or attitude. For instance, a person might sit or stand with a straight back and shoulders to convey confidence and authority. Yet, subtle shifts in posture can betray anxiety or discomfort, particularly in high-pressure situations. Mehrabian (1972) explores the dual nature of posture, noting how it can be both a consciously controlled and an unconsciously revealing aspect of nonverbal communication.

Innate *vs.* Learned Nonverbal Behaviors

The distinction between innate and learned nonverbal behaviors is critical in understanding the origins and meanings of these signals. Some nonverbal behaviors appear to be universal and biologically ingrained, while others are shaped by cultural norms and social learning. Innate nonverbal behaviors are those that seem to be hardwired into the human experience. Charles Darwin, in 1872, in his seminal work *The Expression of the Emotions in Man and Animals*, argued that certain facial expressions, such as smiling when happy or frowning when sad, are universal across all human cultures. These expressions are not learned but are instead natural responses to emotional stimuli, reflecting the deep evolutionary roots of human communication (Noroozi *et al.*, 2021).

In contrast, learned nonverbal behaviors are those that vary significantly across cultures and are acquired through socialization. The 'OK' hand gesture, for instance, is a positive sign in some cultures but can be offensive in others, illustrating the cultural specificity of some nonverbal signals. Hall (1966) explored these cultural differences extensively, showing how gestures, personal space, and other aspects of nonverbal communication are learned behaviors that vary widely depending on societal norms and values.

CULTURAL INFLUENCES ON NONVERBAL COMMUNICATION

Cultural context plays a pivotal role in shaping how nonverbal communication is both expressed and interpreted. The same gesture or expression can have vastly different meanings in different cultural settings, making it essential to consider cultural influences when analyzing nonverbal behavior. One significant area of cultural variation is proxemics, the study of personal space. Hall (1966) introduced the concept of proxemics, identifying different distance zones that people maintain in social interactions: intimate, personal, social, and public. What is considered an appropriate distance in one culture might be perceived as intrusive or distant in another. For example, cultures with a preference for close personal space might view a step back as a sign of discomfort or disinterest, whereas cultures that value more personal space might see the same gesture as a natural boundary.

Similarly, haptics, or communication through touch, vary greatly across cultures. Haptics, or communication through touch, vary significantly across cultures, with some cultures viewing touch as a warm gesture and others perceiving it as intrusive or inappropriate in certain contexts. As Peter Andersen (2008) explains, the acceptability and interpretation of touch are deeply embedded in cultural norms, which play a pivotal role in shaping how messages through touch are perceived and understood across different cultural contexts.

Another area of cultural variation is oculesics, which focuses on eye behavior, including eye contact, gaze direction, and pupil dilation. In some cultures, direct eye contact is seen as a sign of confidence and attentiveness, while in others, it may be considered disrespectful or confrontational. Argyle and Cook (1976) examine the role of eye contact in nonverbal communication, noting its cultural variability and its impact on social interactions.

Factors Affecting Nonverbal Communication

Nonverbal communication is influenced by a variety of factors that shape how individuals express and interpret nonverbal cues. These factors, including gender, age, personality, and emotional state, play a critical role in determining the nuances of body language, facial expressions, and spatial behavior. Understanding these influences can provide insights into the diverse ways people convey emotions, establish connections, and communicate intentions nonverbally. Academic research highlights that nonverbal communication patterns are not only shaped by situational contexts but also deeply embedded in individual differences and developmental factors.

For instance, gender-related differences often reveal how men and women may express emotions and respond to nonverbal cues in distinct ways. Similarly, age impacts nonverbal behaviors as children, adults, and older individuals develop different expressive styles and levels of emotional control. Personality traits also play a significant role, with characteristics such as extroversion or introversion influencing the degree of physical openness or reservedness in body language. Additionally, emotional states can instantly alter nonverbal expressions, with signs of anxiety or confidence visibly displayed in gestures, eye contact, and posture. This section explores these key factors to shed light on how individual and contextual variables shape nonverbal communication, contributing to the complexity and richness of human interaction (Harrigan *et al.*, 2005; Knapp *et al.*, 2013; Lakin, 2006; Manusov & Patterson, 2006):

Gender Differences

Gender differences in nonverbal communication have been widely studied. Research suggests that women tend to be more expressive and better at reading nonverbal cues, particularly facial expressions. Men, on average, tend to use more space and engage in more territory-marking behaviors.

Age-related Changes

Age-related changes in nonverbal communication are also notable. Children tend to be more openly expressive, while adults often learn to modulate their expressions based on social norms. Older adults may show decreased expressiveness due to physiological changes.

Personality Traits

Personality traits significantly influence nonverbal behavior. Extroverts, for instance, tend to use more expansive gestures and maintain closer interpersonal distances compared to introverts.

Emotional State

Emotional state profoundly affects nonverbal communication. Anxiety might manifest as fidgeting or avoidance of eye contact, while confidence could be displayed through an open posture and steady gaze.

Applications of Nonverbal Communication Research

The study of nonverbal communication extends beyond theoretical understanding, providing practical applications across various professional fields. By decoding the subtleties of nonverbal cues, professionals in psychology, law enforcement, business, education, and healthcare can enhance their effectiveness in their respective domains. This section explores how nonverbal communication research is applied in these fields, demonstrating its broad relevance and utility, as shown in Fig. (**5**):

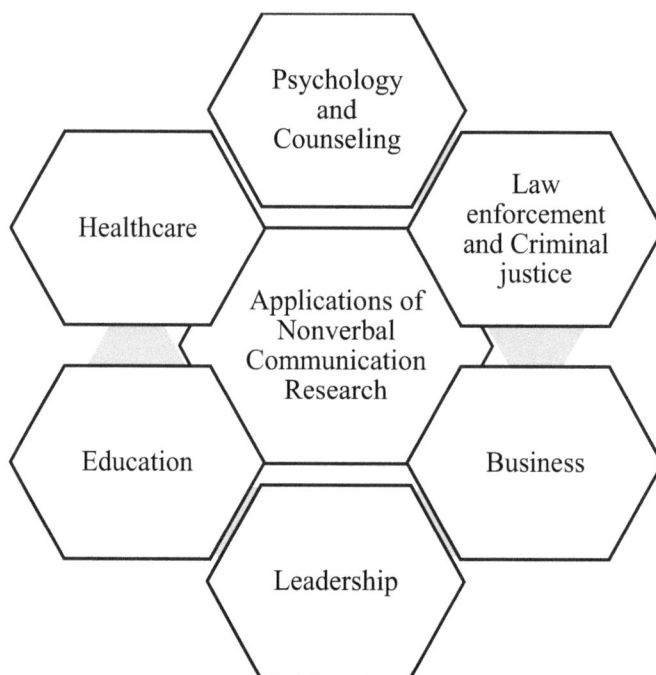

Fig. (5). Applications of nonverbal communication research. Source:Adapted fromHall *et al.* (2019); Egan (2013); Vrij (2008); Ekman (2009); Thompson *et al.* (2010); Goman (2011); Maroni *et al.* (2008); Mehrabian (2007); Ambady *et al.* (2002); Hall *et al.* (1995); Roter & Hall (2006).

Psychology and Counseling

In the field of psychology and counseling, nonverbal communication plays a critical role in understanding and interpreting clients' emotions, thoughts, and intentions. Therapists often rely on nonverbal cues—such as body language, facial expressions, and tone of voice—to gauge their clients' emotional states, especially when clients struggle to articulate their feelings verbally (Hall *et al.*, 2019). For instance, a client might say they are "fine," but their slumped posture, lack of eye contact, and fidgeting hands may indicate anxiety or discomfort. By recognizing these nonverbal signals, therapists can respond more empathetically and provide the appropriate support. Furthermore, therapists can use their own nonverbal behaviors, such as maintaining eye contact, nodding, or adopting an open posture, to build rapport and create a sense of trust and safety for their clients (Egan, 2013).

Law Enforcement and Criminal Justice

In law enforcement and criminal justice, the ability to accurately interpret nonverbal communication is essential, particularly in situations involving interrogation and deception detection. Officers and investigators are trained to observe nonverbal cues that might indicate stress, evasion, or dishonesty. For example, a suspect's inconsistent eye movements, nervous fidgeting, or sudden changes in posture might signal discomfort or deceit (Vrij, 2008). Research in this area has led to the development of techniques such as the Behavioral Analysis Interview (BAI), which uses both verbal and nonverbal indicators to assess the credibility of a suspect's statements. However, it's important to note that while nonverbal cues can provide valuable insights, they must be interpreted with caution and within the context of other evidence, as they are not foolproof indicators of truthfulness (Ekman, 2009).

Business

In the business world, nonverbal communication is a powerful tool that can enhance negotiation skills, improve sales techniques, and foster effective leadership. Successful negotiators, for instance, are adept at reading their counterparts' nonverbal signals, such as micro-expressions of doubt or discomfort, which can inform strategic decisions during negotiations (Thompson *et al.*, 2010). Sales professionals also benefit from understanding nonverbal communication, as it enables them to better gauge customer interest and tailor their approach accordingly. For example, a customer's body language—such as leaning in, nodding, or maintaining strong eye contact—can indicate engagement and readiness to purchase, while crossed arms or averted gaze might suggest hesitation or disinterest.

Leadership

Leadership, too, is deeply intertwined with nonverbal communication. Leaders who are aware of their own nonverbal signals, such as posture, gestures, and tone, can inspire confidence, convey authority, and build strong relationships with their teams. Additionally, understanding the nonverbal cues of others allows leaders to respond to team members' unspoken concerns and foster a supportive, collaborative environment (Goman, 2011).

Education

Educators can leverage nonverbal communication to create more effective and engaging learning environments. Nonverbal cues such as gestures, facial expressions, and eye contact can be powerful tools in classroom management and student engagement. For instance, teachers who maintain eye contact and use expressive gestures are more likely to capture students' attention and convey enthusiasm for the subject matter, which in turn can enhance students' motivation to learn (Maroni *et al.*, 2008). Additionally, educators can use nonverbal communication to manage classroom dynamics. A teacher's use of proximity, for example, can signal authority and keep students on task, while a smile or nod can provide positive reinforcement. Understanding students' nonverbal behaviors is also crucial, as it can help educators identify when students are confused, disengaged, or in need of additional support, even if they do not verbalize these feelings (Mehrabian, 2007).

Healthcare

In healthcare, nonverbal communication is essential for building patient rapport, understanding concerns, and improving diagnoses. Physicians and healthcare providers who are skilled at reading nonverbal cues—such as facial expressions, body language, and tone of voice—can gain a deeper understanding of their patients' emotional states and concerns, even when these are not explicitly expressed (Ambady *et al.*, 2002). For example, a patient's hesitation to maintain eye contact or a tense posture might indicate anxiety or discomfort, prompting the physician to explore these feelings further. Additionally, nonverbal communication is vital in situations where patients are unable to communicate verbally, such as in cases of severe illness, cognitive impairment, or language barriers. In these instances, healthcare providers must rely heavily on nonverbal signals to assess pain, discomfort, and emotional well-being (Hall *et al.*, 1995). Effective nonverbal communication can also enhance patient satisfaction and adherence to treatment plans. In healthcare, nonverbal communication is crucial, especially in patient care. Studies show that nonverbal cues like eye contact and touch can improve patient satisfaction and trust, leading to better adherence to treatment plans (Roter & Hall, 2006).

SCIENTIFIC   METHODS   IN   STUDYING   NONVERBAL COMMUNICATION

The study of nonverbal communication is a multidisciplinary endeavor that draws upon a variety of scientific methods to explore how humans convey and interpret meaning through behaviors other than spoken words. From early observational techniques to cutting-edge technological tools, researchers have developed a range of approaches to systematically analyze nonverbal cues. These methods are crucial for advancing our understanding of the subtle yet powerful forms of communication that occur beyond the spoken word.

Observational Studies

Observational studies have long been the foundation of research into nonverbal communication. These studies typically involve the systematic observation and coding of nonverbal behaviors in natural or semi-natural settings. By carefully recording and analyzing interactions, researchers can identify patterns and correlations between specific nonverbal behaviors and social outcomes. In the area of nonverbal communication, naturalistic observation is particularly valuable because it allows researchers to study behaviors as they occur spontaneously in real-world contexts. For example, early work by Birdwhistell (1970), a pioneer in the field of kinesics, involved detailed observations of body movements, gestures, and facial expressions across different cultures. Birdwhistell's approach was grounded in the belief that much of human communication is conveyed through these nonverbal channels, often without conscious awareness. Observational methods can be both qualitative and quantitative. Qualitative observations might involve detailed descriptions of how individuals use space, touch, or eye contact in different social settings, providing rich, contextual insights. Quantitative observational studies, on the other hand, involve coding specific behaviors and counting their occurrences to test hypotheses statistically. For instance, researchers might quantify the frequency of smiles during a conversation to explore the relationship between nonverbal behavior and social bonding.

Experimental Research

While observational studies offer valuable insights into naturalistic behaviors, experimental research provides the control necessary to isolate and examine specific nonverbal cues in detail. Through controlled experiments, researchers can manipulate variables and measure their effects on participants' perceptions, emotions, or behaviors. One common experimental approach involves manipulating nonverbal cues such as gestures, facial expressions, or posture and then assessing how these changes affect observers' interpretations. For example, a study might involve showing participants images or videos of people displaying different facial expressions and then asking them to rate the emotions they perceive. This type of research has been instrumental in understanding the impact of nonverbal cues on social judgments, such as trustworthiness or attractiveness. Experimental methods are particularly useful for testing theories about the functions of specific nonverbal behaviors. For example, research has shown that certain nonverbal cues, such as open-body postures or direct eye contact, can influence perceptions of dominance or leadership (Carney *et al.*, 2010). By systematically varying these cues in experimental settings, researchers can draw conclusions about their causal effects on social interaction.

Technological Advancements

Technological advancements have revolutionized the field. In recent years, technological advancements have significantly expanded the tools available for studying nonverbal communication, enabling researchers to capture and analyze nonverbal cues with unprecedented precision. These innovations are transforming the field by providing objective, quantifiable data that can complement traditional observational and experimental methods:

Facial Recognition and Micro-Expression Detection

One of the most significant technological advancements in this area is the development of facial recognition software. These systems can automatically detect and categorize facial expressions, even capturing micro-expressions—brief, involuntary facial movements that reveal genuine emotions. This technology has been particularly valuable in fields such as psychology and security, where understanding true emotional states is critical. For instance, studies using such software have revealed that micro-expressions can be reliable indicators of deceit or concealed emotions, offering new avenues for research into honesty and emotional regulation.

Eye-Tracking Technology

Eye-tracking devices have revolutionized the study of oculesics, or eye behavior, by providing precise data on where, when, and how long individuals focus their gaze during interactions. This technology allows researchers to explore how visual attention is directed in social situations, shedding light on the importance of eye contact, gaze patterns, and visual attention in communication. For example, eye-tracking studies have demonstrated that people tend to fixate more on the eyes and mouth when trying to interpret emotions, highlighting the significance of these facial features in nonverbal communication (Duchowski, 2007).

Thermal Imaging

Another cutting-edge tool in the study of nonverbal communication is thermal imaging, which detects subtle changes in facial blood flow that are associated with emotional arousal. When a person experiences strong emotions, such as stress, fear, or excitement, these emotions can trigger physiological responses that alter blood flow, leading to changes in facial temperature. Thermal imaging technology can capture these changes, providing a non-invasive method for studying the physiological components of emotional responses in real time (Ioannou *et al.*, 2014). This technique is particularly useful for exploring the connection between nonverbal cues and underlying emotional states.

CHALLENGES IN INTERPRETING NONVERBAL CUES

Interpreting nonverbal cues involves navigating challenges like cultural differences, situational context, and individual expressions, making it prone to misinterpretation. Subtle variations in gestures or facial expressions can hold distinct meanings across cultures, while emotional states further complicate accurate decoding. Some of the major challenges in interpreting nonverbal cues shown in Fig. (**6**) are explained as follows (Burgoon *et al.*, 2016; Ekman & Friesen, 1975; Hall, 1976; Mehrabian, 1972):

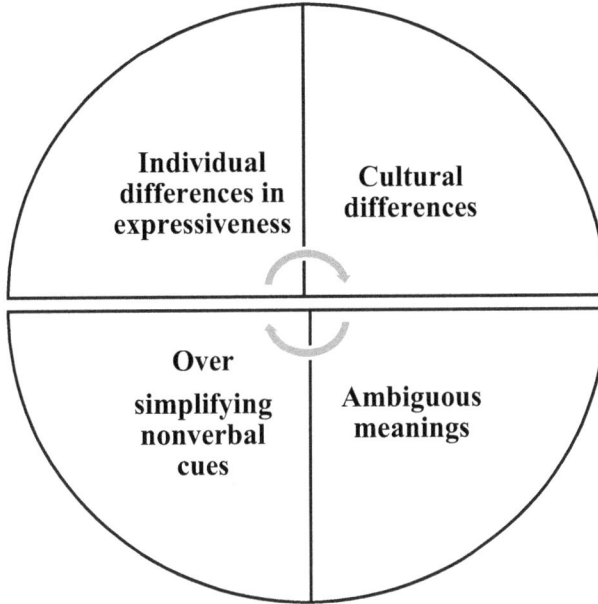

Fig. (6). Challenges in interpreting nonverbal cues. Source: Burgoon *et al.* (2016); Ekman & Friesen (1975); Hall (1976); Mehrabian (1972).

Individual differences in expressiveness can significantly impact the interpretation of nonverbal cues. People vary in how they express emotions nonverbally, influenced by factors such as personality, emotional regulation, and psychological states. For example, some individuals may be more expressive with their facial expressions, while others might rely more on gestures or tone of voice. This variability can lead to misinterpretations if one assumes that all individuals use nonverbal cues in the same way (Ekman & Friesen, 1975).

Cultural differences play a crucial role in the interpretation of nonverbal cues. What is considered an appropriate gesture or expression in one culture might be interpreted differently in another. For instance, while direct eye contact is seen as a sign of confidence in many Western cultures, it might be perceived as rude or confrontational in some Asian cultures (Hall, 1976). This variation underscores the importance of understanding cultural context when interpreting nonverbal communication.

The context in which nonverbal cues are displayed is essential for accurate interpretation. Nonverbal behaviors can carry different meanings depending on the setting—what might be interpreted as friendliness in a casual environment could be seen as unprofessional in a formal setting. For example, a casual gesture like a pat on the back might be appropriate among friends but could be considered inappropriate or intrusive in a professional environment (Burgoon *et al.*, 2016).

Oversimplifying nonverbal cues by assuming a direct one-to-one correspondence between specific behaviors and emotions can lead to inaccuracies. Nonverbal communication is often multifaceted, and multiple cues need to be considered together with verbal content and context. For example, a person's crossed arms might be interpreted as defensive, but this could also indicate discomfort, cold, or simply a relaxed posture, depending on the situation (Mehrabian, 1972).

CONCLUSION

The science of nonverbal communication reveals the complex and nuanced ways humans interact beyond words. From the subtle raise of an eyebrow to the unconscious mirroring of another's posture, these silent signals form an intricate dance of communication that occurs in every human interaction. As we have explored in this chapter, nonverbal communication is deeply rooted in our biology, shaped by our culture, and influenced by individual differences. It plays a crucial role in complementing, emphasizing, and sometimes contradicting our verbal messages. Understanding the science behind nonverbal communication equips us with valuable tools for better interpersonal communication, improved empathy, and more effective social interactions. As we move further into the digital age, where face-to-face interactions are often replaced by screens, the ability to read and interpret nonverbal cues becomes even more critical. The field of nonverbal communication continues to evolve, with new technologies offering unprecedented insights into the subtleties of human expression and behavior. As we uncover more about this "silent language," we gain a deeper appreciation for the complexity and richness of human communication. By honing our skills in reading and using nonverbal cues, we can enhance our personal and professional relationships, becoming more effective communicators and more empathetic human beings. The magic gaze, indeed, holds the power to unlock the unspoken thoughts and emotions that color our daily interactions. Emerging technologies like virtual and augmented reality offer new avenues for studying nonverbal communication in controlled yet realistic environments. Cross-cultural studies are becoming increasingly important in our globalized world, helping to distinguish universal nonverbal behaviors from culturally specific ones. The integration of artificial intelligence in nonverbal communication research is promising. AI can potentially analyze vast amounts of nonverbal data, identifying patterns too subtle for human observers to detect.

Class Activity: "Silent Storytelling"

In the "Silent Storytelling" activity, participants work in pairs to convey and guess scenarios using only nonverbal cues. This exercise enhances their awareness of body language and facial expressions as they explore the effectiveness and challenges of communicating without words. The activity fosters a deeper understanding of how nonverbal communication can convey meaning in various contexts.

Duration: 30 minutes

Materials needed: Timer, list of simple scenarios

Instructions:

1. Divide participants into pairs.
2. Provide each pair with a simple scenario (*e.g.*, "asking for directions," "ordering at a restaurant," "comforting a friend").
3. One person in each pair has 2 minutes to convey the scenario without using words.
4. The other person tries to guess the scenario based solely on nonverbal cues.
5. Pairs switch roles and repeat with a new scenario.
6. After 3-4 rounds, gather as a group to discuss:
   - Which nonverbal cues were most effective in conveying meaning?
   - What challenges did they face in communicating without words?
   - How did this exercise heighten their awareness of nonverbal communication?

CHAPTER 2

Understanding Eye Movements and Micro-Expressions

Abstract: This chapter unravels the complexities of eye movements and micro-expressions, delving into how these subtle cues reflect our true emotions and intentions. Eye behavior, including eye contact, blinking, and gaze aversion, plays a pivotal role in communication, with eye-tracking studies revealing how attention and focus can be deciphered. Micro-expressions, which are fleeting, involuntary facial movements, provide a window into concealed emotions, often escaping conscious control. The chapter explains the science behind these expressions and discusses how they can be detected and interpreted in various contexts, such as negotiation, security, and psychological analysis. By exploring both scientific theories and practical applications, readers will learn to recognize and analyze these subtle cues to gain deeper insights into people's feelings and thoughts. Emphasis is placed on how cultural differences may affect the interpretation of eye behavior and micro-expressions, making cultural awareness crucial. Real-world examples and exercises offer opportunities for readers to sharpen their observational skills and apply this knowledge effectively.

Keywords: Emotion detection, Eye movements, Gaze behavior, Micro-expressions, Pupil dilation.

INTRODUCTION

The eyes are often called the "windows to the soul," and for good reason. They play a crucial role in nonverbal communication, conveying a wealth of information about our thoughts, emotions, and intentions (Oggiano, 2023). This chapter explores the intricate world of eye movements and micro-expressions, as shown in Fig. (**1**), exploring how these subtle cues can reveal what words often conceal.

THE ANATOMY OF THE EYE IN COMMUNICATION

Understanding ocular communication requires a grasp of the anatomy of the eye and how its various components contribute to nonverbal signaling. The eye's

Yuvika Singh

structure plays a crucial role in how we convey and interpret emotions, intentions, and cognitive states (Heiting, 2019).

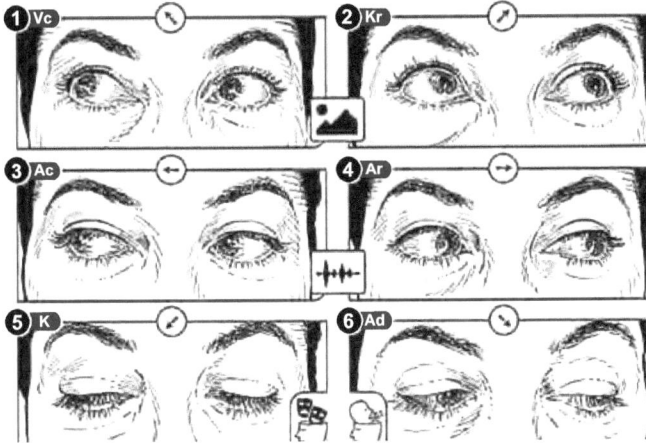

Fig. (1). Eye movements. Source: Oggiano (2023).

This section explores the anatomical features of the eye and their significance in communication. The iris, pupil, sclera (white of the eye), and the surrounding muscles all play roles in conveying information:

Pupil Dilation

Pupil dilation is a key aspect of ocular communication. The pupil, the black part of the eye, adjusts its size in response to light levels, but it also changes with emotional and cognitive states, as shown in Fig. (**2**):

Interest and Arousal

Research has shown that pupils dilate in response to emotional arousal. For example, when a person is interested or excited, their pupils may dilate (Kahneman & Beatty, 1966). This physiological response is often subconscious and can provide insight into a person's level of engagement or attraction.

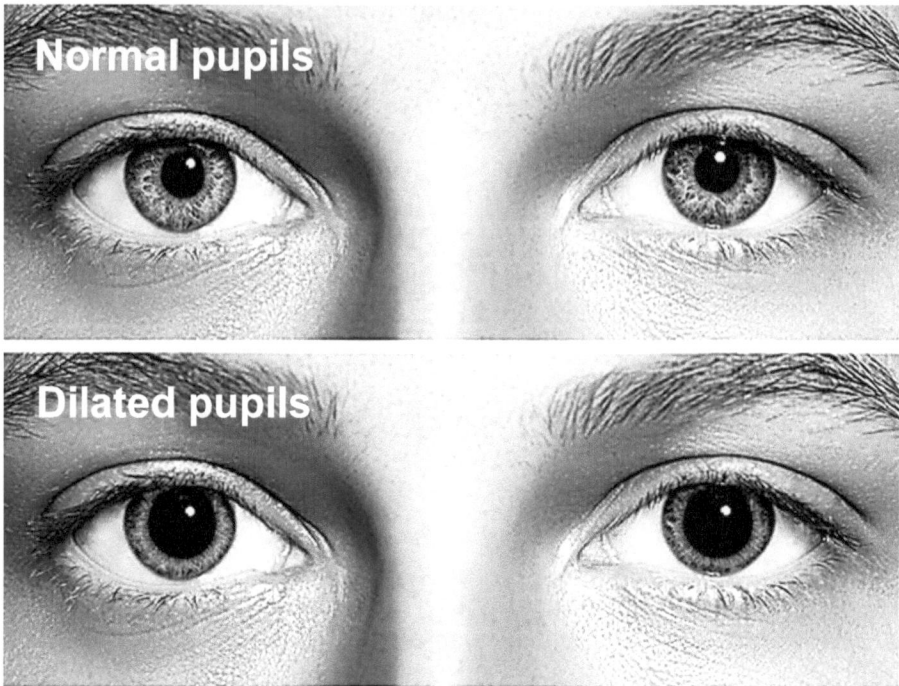

Fig. (2). Normal and dilated pupils. Source: Ekman & Friesen (1975); Heiting (2019); Kahneman & Beatty (1966); Spector (1990).

Cognitive Load

Pupil size can also reflect cognitive load. Studies by Spector (1990) indicate that when a person is engaged in complex mental tasks, their pupils tend to dilate. This is thought to be due to increased cognitive effort and arousal.

Sclera

Sclera, or the white part of the eye, is not merely a protective outer layer but also plays a role in communication:

Emotional States

Changes in sclera visibility can indicate emotional states. For instance, increased sclera visibility due to wide-open eyes might suggest surprise or fear, while reduced visibility from squinting could indicate suspicion or confusion (Ekman & Friesen, 1975).

Direction of Attention

The sclera also helps indicate where attention is directed. When someone looks in a certain direction, the visible sclera can reveal the focus of their attention or interest. For example, if someone is looking away from you, the increased sclera visibility can indicate disengagement or disinterest.

Eye Muscles

They control movements like blinking, squinting, and widening, each carrying potential meaning.

EYE MOVEMENTS

Eye movements are complex and can reveal a great deal about cognitive processes and emotional states. Let's explore deeper into the types of eye movements (Frischen *et al.*, 2007; Gilchrist, 2011):

Saccades

These are rapid, ballistic movements of the eyes that abruptly change the point of fixation. They range in duration from 10 to 100 milliseconds. Saccades are used to scan a visual scene, and the pattern of these movements can indicate what a person finds interesting or important in their environment. For instance, when looking at a face, people typically make saccades between the eyes, nose, and mouth - the most informative areas for social interaction.

Understanding **saccades** and their patterns is highly valuable in various fields, especially for gaining insights into attention, perception, and behavior. Here is how saccades are helpful (Frischen *et al.*, 2007; Gilchrist, 2011; Rayner, 1998):

Psychology and Neuroscience

Saccades show where our visual focus lies. By tracking these eye movements, researchers can see which parts of a visual scene or object are most important to us, revealing what captures attention. Patterns of saccades can indicate cognitive processing. For instance, frequent shifts in gaze could show that a person is engaged in deeper analysis or problem-solving.

Social Interaction

When looking at a face, people typically focus on the eyes, nose, and mouth, as these areas provide key social information such as emotions, intentions, and reactions. Tracking saccades helps understand how people interpret non-verbal cues and social signals during conversations. By analyzing saccade patterns, it is possible to study how individuals with social disorders, such as autism, engage with social stimuli differently, leading to better therapeutic approaches.

Marketing and Design

In marketing and web design, saccades help measure where a person's attention is focused on a webpage, ad, or product. Understanding these patterns allows companies to optimize layouts and make key information more visible, improving user engagement. Saccade tracking can reveal which elements of an advertisement draw the most attention, helping marketers place important information like logos, promotions, or calls to action more effectively.

Education

Saccades play a role in how we read and learn. Tracking these movements can help identify reading difficulties, like dyslexia, as students may show different saccade patterns when struggling with text.

Medical Diagnostics

Abnormal saccade patterns can indicate issues with the brain's visual or motor systems, helping diagnose conditions like Parkinson's disease or multiple sclerosis. They can also reflect the effects of head injuries or cognitive decline. Saccade analysis can aid in diagnosing visual disorders and help refine treatment approaches for people with impaired visual tracking or focus.

Smooth Pursuit

This type of eye movement allows the eyes to closely follow a moving object. It's much slower than a saccade and requires a moving target to activate. The accuracy of smooth pursuit can be affected by factors like attention, expectation, and the predictability of the target's motion. Impaired smooth pursuit is sometimes associated with neurological or psychiatric conditions. These movements play a crucial role in both daily life and various fields of study. Here is how smooth pursuit tracking is helpful (Duchowski, 2007):

Neurology and Psychiatry

Impaired smooth pursuit movements can be an indicator of neurological conditions like Parkinson's disease, Alzheimer's, multiple sclerosis, and even schizophrenia. Doctors often use smooth pursuit tests to assess brain function and diagnose these conditions early. Smooth pursuit involves coordination between different brain regions, including those responsible for vision, motor control, and prediction. Irregularities in smooth pursuit can reveal problems in these areas, providing insight into brain health.

Psychology and Cognitive Research

Smooth pursuit requires focused attention on a moving target. Researchers can use it to study how well people maintain attention and track objects, helping us understand how attention works under different conditions. Factors like mental workload or multitasking can affect smooth pursuit accuracy. By measuring this, researchers can assess how cognitive demands influence eye movements, shedding light on mental processes.

Sports Performance

Athletes rely heavily on smooth pursuits to follow fast-moving objects (like a ball) in sports such as tennis, baseball, or soccer. Studying smooth pursuit can help optimize performance and enhance training strategies to improve visual tracking. Accurate, smooth pursuit enhances the ability to react to moving targets quickly and efficiently. Improving these movements can translate into better performance in sports and other activities that require quick responses.

Vision Therapy and Rehabilitation

For people with visual or coordination disorders, therapies that target smooth pursuit can improve their ability to follow objects and maintain focus. This can be helpful for conditions like strabismus (eye misalignment) or after a stroke that affects vision. Children with developmental delays or learning disorders may show poor smooth pursuit abilities, and tracking these movements can help diagnose and provide targeted interventions.

Virtual Reality and Gaming

In VR and gaming, understanding smooth pursuit can lead to more realistic environments by helping track how users follow moving objects. This makes for a more immersive experience where the system adapts based on where the player is looking. In fields like augmented reality (AR) and virtual reality (VR), smooth pursuit eye tracking can enhance user interfaces, allowing computers to respond to where the user's eyes are focused. This could lead to more natural and intuitive control systems.

Driving and Safety

When driving, smooth pursuit helps drivers track moving objects such as cars, pedestrians, or cyclists. Impaired smooth pursuit can reduce the ability to react to such hazards, making it a critical function for road safety. Smooth pursuit eye tracking can also be used in tests to detect fatigue or impairment (due to alcohol or drugs) in drivers. Diminished smooth pursuit capabilities are often an early indicator of tiredness or intoxication.

Aging and Vision

Smooth pursuit tends to decline with age, affecting how older adults track moving objects. Studying this decline can help develop interventions to maintain visual tracking abilities, contributing to better quality of life for aging populations.

Fixations

Fixations are the pauses between saccades, where the eyes are relatively stationary. Fixations typically last between 200-300 milliseconds. The location and duration of fixations can provide insight into what information a person is processing. For example, longer fixations often indicate deeper processing or difficulty extracting information. Here is how fixations are helpful across different fields (Duchowski, 2017; Henderson, 2003; Holmqvist *et al.*, 2011; Just & Carpenter, 1976; Rayner, 1998):

Understanding Attention and Cognitive Processing

Longer fixations often indicate that a person is focusing more on a particular piece of information, suggesting deeper cognitive processing. For instance, when reading a difficult sentence or viewing a complex image, longer fixations occur as the brain works harder to understand the material. The locations where fixations occur can reveal what people find most interesting or relevant in a scene. By tracking these points, researchers can understand which elements capture attention, providing insight into what stands out or requires more focus.

Reading Research

Fixation patterns are often used to study reading behavior. Longer fixations may signal difficulty in reading, such as when someone encounters an unfamiliar word or concept. In contrast, shorter, efficient fixations can indicate fluency and ease in reading. Fixation analysis is helpful for identifying reading disorders like dyslexia. Children or adults with dyslexia tend to have longer, irregular fixations and more frequent regressions (re-reading), indicating difficulty processing text.

Marketing and Advertising

In marketing, fixations help businesses understand what parts of an advertisement, website, or product design attract the most attention. This information can guide design improvements, ensuring that important information (like pricing or product features) is placed in areas where viewers tend to fixate. Studying fixations can reveal the factors that drive consumer behavior. For example, longer fixations on certain products or features in an ad may suggest higher interest or deeper consideration, helping marketers tailor their strategies.

Human-Computer Interaction and UX Design

Fixation patterns in user experience (UX) research show how users interact with websites or apps. Longer fixations on navigation menus, buttons, or forms may indicate confusion or difficulty finding information. This insight helps designers improve layout and functionality for a better user experience. By analyzing where users fixate on a screen, designers can adjust content placement and design to make it more intuitive and engaging. Fixation analysis ensures key information is seen and absorbed quickly.

Sports and Performance

In sports, fixation patterns help players focus on important elements, like a ball's movement, an opponent's body language, or the position of other players. Training fixation behavior can improve athletes' awareness and reaction times. Athletes with more efficient fixation patterns tend to perform better as they process relevant information more quickly and accurately. Coaches can use fixation analysis to fine-tune players' visual strategies.

Neurological and Psychological Diagnosis

Fixations can reveal how much cognitive load someone is experiencing. For instance, during tasks requiring heavy mental effort, people tend to fixate longer on challenging sections. This can be used in psychological and neurological assessments to measure attention, stress, or difficulty levels. Studying fixations helps researchers understand how visual memory works. Longer fixations might occur when someone is trying to recall information, as their brain processes and integrates what they are seeing with what they remember.

Education and Learning

In educational research, fixation patterns can indicate how students engage with learning materials. For example, a student who fixates more on diagrams rather than text might benefit from visual learning methods, while another who focuses on text might prefer reading-based approaches. Teachers can design materials to guide student fixations to key areas that require more focus, helping improve learning outcomes.

Virtual Reality (VR) and Gaming

Fixation tracking in VR and gaming helps developers create more engaging environments by understanding where players look and what captures their attention. It ensures that key game elements are positioned where players are most likely to notice them. In VR, fixation-based interaction allows users to select or manipulate objects just by looking at them. This makes the experience more intuitive, reducing the need for additional input devices.

GAZE PATTERNS AND THEIR MEANINGS

Gaze patterns reflect how individuals use eye movements to communicate attention, emotions, and intentions. These patterns, including direct eye contact, gaze aversion, and scanning, play a vital role in nonverbal communication and vary based on cultural, situational, and psychological factors. Research indicates that gaze behavior is closely linked to cognitive and affective processes (Rayner, 1998; Henderson, 2003) (Fig. **3**).

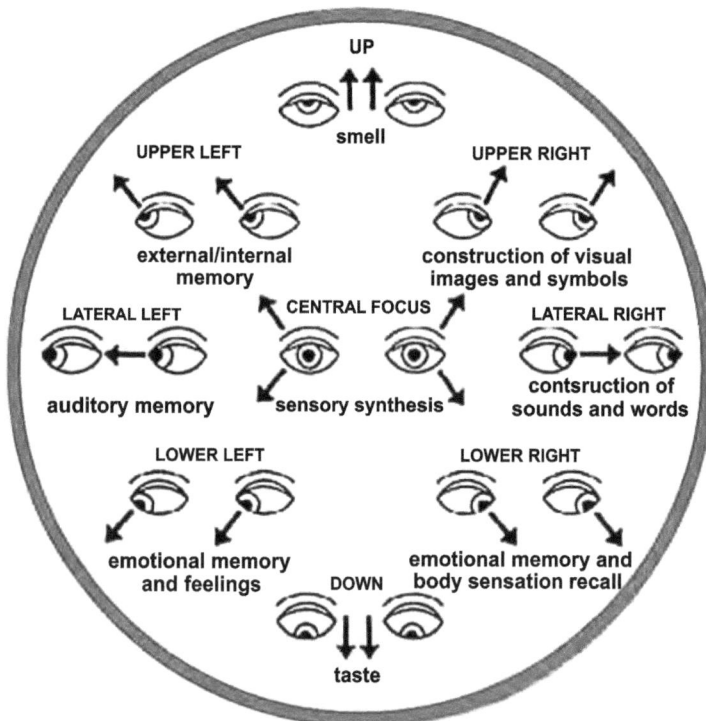

Fig. (3). Emotions through the eyes. Source:Adapted from Argyle & Cook (1976); Kleinke (1986); Rayner (1998); Vrij (2008).

Direct Gaze

Maintaining eye contact can indicate attention, confidence, or a desire to communicate. However, the appropriate duration of direct gaze varies culturally. In many Western cultures, intermittent direct gaze is expected in conversation, while in some East Asian cultures, prolonged direct gaze can be seen as disrespectful. Studies suggest that direct eye contact enhances the perception of trustworthiness and dominance in social interactions (Kleinke, 1986).

Here's how different cultures interpret and use eye contact:

(e.g., North America, Europe)

Direct eye contact is often seen as a sign of confidence, honesty, and respect (Argyle & Cook, 1976). In conversations, maintaining intermittent eye contact is expected, particularly in professional or social contexts. Avoiding eye contact can be perceived as disinterest, dishonesty, or lack of confidence. People tend to use moderate to high levels of direct eye contact, with intermittent breaks. Eye contact is encouraged during conversations, presentations, and even casual interactions as it reflects attentiveness (Kleinke, 1986).

East Asian Cultures (e.g., Japan, China, Korea)

In some East Asian cultures, prolonged direct eye contact can be perceived as aggressive, confrontational, or disrespectful, particularly in hierarchical or formal settings (Kleinke, 1986). Avoiding direct eye contact is often a sign of respect, especially when interacting with elders or authority figures (Argyle & Cook, 1976). People may deliberately avoid prolonged eye contact to show deference or politeness, especially in professional environments. Brief glances, rather than sustained eye contact, are more common.

Middle Eastern Cultures

Direct eye contact is often considered important for establishing trust and credibility. It shows interest and sincerity in conversations (Argyle & Cook, 1976). However, cultural norms also dictate that direct gaze can vary based on gender interactions, with more conservative practices in place between men and women. Men are expected to maintain direct eye contact during interactions with other men as a sign of honesty and respect. However, when interacting with women, depending on the level of conservatism, eye contact may be more restrained (Kleinke, 1986).

African Cultures

In many African cultures, direct eye contact can signal disrespect when made with elders or authority figures (Argyle & Cook, 1976). In contrast, in peer-to-peer or casual settings, direct eye contact may be more acceptable. Younger individuals may avoid direct eye contact with their elders as a show of humility or respect, while eye contact among peers or in relaxed settings might be more prevalent (Kleinke, 1986).

Latin American Cultures

Direct eye contact is generally viewed as important for building personal connections. It reflects interest, sincerity, and respect (Kleinke, 1986). However, staring or prolonged eye contact can be interpreted as invasive or challenging. Latin Americans often use moderate levels of eye contact in personal and business settings, emphasizing warmth and openness. Too little eye contact can come across as indifferent, but too much may seem confrontational (Argyle & Cook, 1976).

South Asian Cultures (e.g., India, Pakistan)

Like East Asian cultures, South Asian countries often view prolonged eye contact as disrespectful, especially when directed toward elders or authority figures (Kleinke, 1986). Avoiding direct gaze in such contexts signifies respect and submission. While casual eye contact is acceptable among peers, direct gaze is often minimized in formal or hierarchical interactions (Argyle & Cook, 1976).

Averted Gaze

Looking away can indicate discomfort, submission, or lying, but it's also associated with cognitive processing. When people are thinking deeply or trying to recall information, they often look away (Argyle & Cook, 1976; Rayner, 1998; Vrij, 2008).

Western Cultures (e.g., North America, Europe)

In Western cultures, avoiding eye contact or looking away during conversations can often be seen as a sign of discomfort, disinterest, or even dishonesty (Argyle & Cook, 1976; Vrij, 2008). However, people may look away when they are processing thoughts, recalling memories, or imagining scenarios, which are understood as part of cognitive processing (Kleinke, 1986; Rayner, 1998). While an averted gaze is sometimes frowned upon in formal or professional contexts, it is generally accepted as a sign of thinking when people are asked difficult questions. Socially, frequent avoidance of eye contact may still be interpreted as a lack of confidence or engagement.

East Asian Cultures (e.g., Japan, China, Korea)

In many East Asian cultures, averting the gaze—especially with elders or superiors—is a sign of respect rather than avoidance or dishonesty. Maintaining prolonged eye contact is often viewed as confrontational or rude, so looking away is a culturally appropriate way to demonstrate deference and politeness. In hierarchical or formal settings, looking away from direct eye contact can indicate submission and respect. However, averting the gaze in social situations, especially while thinking or recalling information, is common and not seen negatively (Argyle & Cook, 1976).

Middle Eastern Cultures

Direct eye contact is often seen as a sign of sincerity and trustworthiness (Argyle & Cook, 1976; Vrij, 2008). However, frequent averted gaze—especially in the presence of authority figures or during formal interactions—can be interpreted as a lack of confidence or disinterest. In interactions between men and women, averting the gaze may also be a way to adhere to conservative social norms (Kleinke, 1986). Men may maintain eye contact to show respect and engagement, while women may avert their gaze in certain situations as a sign of modesty. In general, an averted gaze during deep thought or cognitive processing is culturally accepted.

African Cultures

In many African cultures, avoiding eye contact with authority figures, elders, or superiors is a sign of humility and respect. An averted gaze is less likely to be interpreted negatively if the social hierarchy is acknowledged. However, in peer-to-peer or casual settings, averted gaze may be seen as evasive or dishonest. Looking away from elders or superiors is expected in formal interactions, but in more casual or personal settings, sustained avoidance of eye contact can create distrust or tension (Rayner, 1998; Vrij, 2008).

Latin American Cultures

In Latin American cultures, eye contact is valued for establishing trust and warmth. However, prolonged eye contact may feel invasive or overly intense. An averted gaze is not typically seen as negative if it occurs while someone is thinking, recalling, or processing information. While direct eye contact is appreciated, an averted gaze during reflection or cognitive processing is generally understood. Avoiding eye contact entirely, however, may signal disinterest or discomfort (Argyle & Cook, 1976).

South Asian Cultures (e.g., India, Pakistan)

In South Asian cultures, particularly in hierarchical or formal contexts, averting the gaze is considered a respectful behavior. It signals submission and humility, especially when interacting with elders or authority figures. However, averting the gaze in social situations might be seen as nervousness or discomfort rather than dishonesty. In professional or formal interactions, an averted gaze may signify respect, but too much avoidance in casual settings could be misinterpreted as a lack of interest or self-confidence (Argyle & Cook, 1976; Rayner, 1998).

DIRECTION OF AVERTED GAZE IN COGNITIVE PROCESSING

Gaze aversion is not just about avoiding eye contact; it can also be linked to cognitive tasks, such as recalling information or emotions (Ekman & Friesen, 1975; Vrij, 2008). While certain gaze directions are often associated with specific cognitive processes, their interpretation varies across cultures, as depicted in Fig. (4).

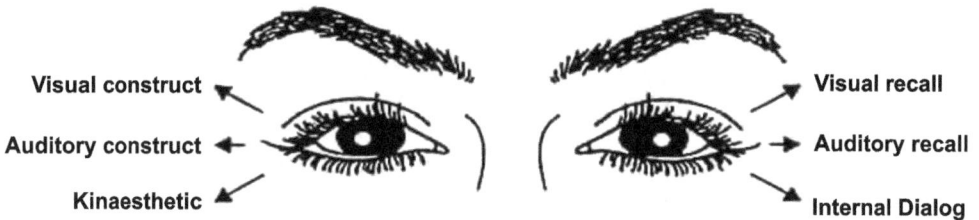

Fig. (4). Telling the truth or lying. Source: Adapted from Argyle & Cook (1976); Ekman & Friesen (1975); Vrij (2008).

Looking up (Visual Recall or Construction)

Western Cultures: Associated with accessing visual memories or constructing images in one's mind. This behavior is generally understood and accepted when someone is asked to remember something.

East Asian Cultures: Though direct eye contact is minimized, looking up while recalling images is generally accepted and not viewed as evasive.

Looking down (Accessing Feelings or Internal Dialogue)

Western Cultures: Often linked to feelings of guilt, sadness, or internal reflection. It may also indicate submission or deference in formal settings.

East Asian Cultures: Frequently interpreted as a sign of respect, particularly in hierarchical relationships. It can also indicate introspection or emotional processing.

Looking Left or Right (Auditory Recall or Construction)

Western Cultures: Looking sideways, either left or right, may indicate someone is recalling sounds, conversations, or information. While it may look evasive to some, it's understood as part of thinking or recalling.

Middle Eastern Cultures: Similar interpretations exist, particularly during cognitive tasks. However, frequent side-glancing may sometimes be perceived as nervousness or avoidance.

Triangular Gaze

In social situations, eyes often move in a triangle between the other person's eyes and mouth. The triangular gaze pattern—where eyes move between the other person's eyes and mouth—is common in social interactions. It helps gauge the other person's expressions and emotions. In Western cultures, this gaze pattern is used to maintain engagement and assess facial expressions. In East Asian cultures, instead of focusing on the eyes, individuals may focus more on the mouth, as direct eye contact is often avoided (Argyle & Cook, 1976).

Upper-left Gaze

When an individual looks to the upper left, it is often associated with recalling visual memories. This involuntary movement occurs when retrieving stored images or past events (Argyle & Cook, 1976).

Upper-right Gaze

A shift in gaze to the upper right is commonly linked with visual construction—mentally imagining or creating something that has not been seen before. This is observed when an individual is being creative, visualizing future events, or forming new scenarios (Vrij, 2008).

Cultural differences significantly influence how gaze patterns are perceived in social interactions. In Western cultures, maintaining intermittent eye contact is often interpreted as a sign of confidence, attention, and honesty. However, in East Asian cultures, prolonged direct gaze can be seen as confrontational or disrespectful, particularly in hierarchical settings. Similarly, in cultures that emphasize respect for elders or authority figures, avoiding eye contact may indicate deference rather than discomfort or dishonesty. These cultural variations highlight the need for context when interpreting nonverbal cues like eye movements, ensuring accurate cross-cultural understanding and communication.

EYE CONTACT: THE POWER OF CONNECTION

Eye contact is indeed a powerful nonverbal tool in human interaction, often communicating far more than words can. It's central to how we connect, understand, and interpret others' intentions and emotions, with nuanced meanings conveyed through its duration, frequency, and context (Hess, 1975; Knapp *et al.*, 2013):

Duration

The length of eye contact can indicate interest, dominance, or discomfort.

Short Glances vs. Extended Gazes: Brief eye contact, lasting around 1-2 seconds, is generally perceived as polite and friendly. However, prolonged eye contact—especially if it goes beyond a few seconds—can convey a range of emotions. Extended eye contact can be strategically used in negotiations to express confidence and assertiveness, signaling interest in the discussion. However, it is important to be mindful of cultural differences and avoid making the other person feel uncomfortable or threatened with excessive gazing.

Averted Gaze: Breaking eye contact or avoiding it during business interactions might suggest that someone is feeling uncertain or disinterested. In contrast, a purposeful averted gaze—such as looking away briefly to think—can demonstrate thoughtfulness and allow space for reflection. In business settings, avoiding eye contact for too long can cause others to perceive a lack of engagement, while maintaining an occasional, purposeful look away can balance attentiveness with composure.

Frequency

How often someone makes eye contact can suggest confidence or anxiety:

High vs. Low Frequency of Eye Contact: Individuals who make frequent eye contact often come across as more self-assured and credible. Regular eye contact is associated with a higher level of engagement and attentiveness, which can help strengthen the speaker-listener relationship. People with lower frequency eye contact may unintentionally appear withdrawn or anxious, as they often avoid eye contact when nervous or uncertain. In a business negotiation, maintaining steady eye contact can establish confidence and trust, whereas, in more intimate settings, too much eye contact may feel intrusive.

Cultural Variations in Frequency: Cultural backgrounds influence how frequently and comfortably people make eye contact. In some cultures, direct and frequent eye contact is considered polite and attentive, while in others, it can be perceived as intrusive or disrespectful. This cultural element is essential to avoid misunderstandings in diverse environments.

Context

The meaning of eye contact varies greatly depending on the situation and relationship (Senna, 2024):

Situational Impact: The context of the interaction profoundly impacts how eye contact is perceived. In formal settings, like a business meeting, eye contact is a sign of respect and professionalism. During social gatherings, it can signal openness and warmth. However, the same level of eye contact may come across differently in personal or intimate contexts.

Relationship Influence: The relationship between individuals plays a significant role in eye contact dynamics. Eye contact with close friends or family tends to be more relaxed, while it may be more regulated in hierarchical relationships, such as between a manager and employee, where too much or too little eye contact could impact perceived authority or respect.

Research shows that eye contact can make individuals appear more credible and persuasive. By maintaining appropriate eye contact, a speaker can enhance their influence over an audience. This is particularly effective in persuasive settings, like interviews or presentations, where eye contact reinforces sincerity and trustworthiness. Eye contact has been shown to improve cognitive function in observers, potentially because it helps maintain focus and engages areas of the brain related to empathy and social processing. When we make eye contact with someone who is explaining a concept, for example, we're more likely to retain and comprehend the information. By understanding these facets of eye contact, we can become more aware of how our gaze affects interactions and can strategically use it to build rapport, convey respect, and establish trust across various settings and relationships.

PUPILLOMETRY: THE TALE TOLD BY PUPIL SIZE

While eye contact offers insights into interpersonal dynamics, another subtle yet informative cue lies in the pupil's response: pupillometry. Pupillometry is the study of pupil size and its changes in response to various stimuli, particularly in relation to emotions, cognitive load, and attention. By examining how the pupil dilates or constricts, researchers can gain insights into a person's emotional state, interest, and mental effort. This subtle but powerful nonverbal cue is often used in psychological studies to understand underlying mental processes and emotional responses. Changes in pupil size, while subtle, can be highly informative (Mathôt, 2018):

Cognitive Load: When we engage in tasks that require intense thinking or mental effort (such as solving complex math problems or learning new concepts), our pupils dilate. This dilation is believed to occur because the brain needs more resources (energy) to process information, and the body responds by increasing the pupil size to take in more visual information.

Emotional Arousal: Emotional stimuli, whether positive (like seeing something you love) or negative (like fear), can cause your pupils to dilate. When we experience strong emotions, our autonomic nervous system (which controls involuntary actions like heart rate and breathing) triggers the pupils to dilate. This happens as part of the body's response to arousal, signaling that we are more alert or excited.

Attraction: When we see someone we are attracted to, our pupils tend to dilate involuntarily. This could be tied to evolutionary biology, as dilated pupils may enhance interpersonal communication by signaling interest, or it could be part of the body's response to the pleasurable feelings associated with attraction.

Decision Making: As we approach a decision point, such as choosing between two options, our pupils can dilate. The dilation reflects mental engagement and indecision as the brain weighs different factors. Studies suggest that pupil size increases just before a decision is made, indicating cognitive effort and the level of uncertainty.

In psychological studies, pupillometry is used to gain insights into cognitive processes and emotional states. For example, pupil size can indicate how much effort someone is putting into understanding or processing information. Marketers use eye-tracking technology to measure pupil responses to advertisements or products. If a product or ad causes pupil dilation, it may suggest that it elicits emotional interest or attraction from viewers, which can help businesses fine-tune their marketing strategies.

MICRO-EXPRESSIONS

Micro-expressions are rapid, involuntary facial expressions that reveal emotions often concealed or repressed. These expressions, which last only fractions of a second, provide a unique window into a person's genuine feelings. Discovered and popularized by psychologist Paul Ekman, they occur universally and consistently across cultures, hinting at their deep evolutionary origins. Ekman identified seven primary micro-expressions—anger, disgust, fear, happiness, sadness, surprise, and contempt—each with specific characteristics that offer insights into underlying emotions, whether openly expressed or hidden (Ekman, 1993; Ekman & Friesen, 1975). Here is an in-depth look at each of these micro-expressions, how they manifest, and their implications:

Anger: Anger is primarily expressed in the eyes and brow area. The eyebrows lower and draw together sharply. The upper eyelids rise, often exposing the sclera, while the lower lids become tense, which can make the eyes look intense and focused. Anger is a strong, action-oriented emotion, often signaling confrontation or resistance. Recognizing anger's subtle emergence is crucial in conflict resolution or de-escalation contexts, as it may indicate growing frustration or disagreement even when the individual tries to appear calm.

Disgust: Disgust typically involves lifting the upper lip and wrinkling the nose. The lower eyelids may push up but remain more relaxed than they are during anger. Disgust is an instinctive reaction to something offensive, whether physically or morally repellent. In interpersonal settings, subtle signs of disgust might reveal hidden dislike or disapproval, even if a person tries to mask their reactions.

Fear: Fear is identifiable by raised upper eyelids, which expose a greater amount of sclera above the iris. The eyebrows are lifted and drawn together, creating a distressed expression. Fear serves as a survival mechanism, alerting others to potential danger or threats. In interviews or security settings, recognizing fear can reveal a subject's anxiety or discomfort, often signaling that they may be hiding something or feeling cornered.

Happiness: Genuine happiness is expressed by the upward drawing of the mouth corners. This expression also involves the raising of the cheeks, which pushes up the lower eyelids and creates "crow's feet" wrinkles around the eyes. Happiness in micro-expressions is an indicator of authentic positive emotion. Unlike fake smiles, which often involve only the mouth, genuine happiness engages the eye area, signaling genuine pleasure or enjoyment. Recognizing true happiness can strengthen connections in social interactions and establish trust.

Sadness: Sadness is marked by the drawing up of the inner corners of the eyebrows, creating a "pinched" appearance. The eyelids often droop slightly, giving the eyes a softened look. Sadness is associated with loss or disappointment. Identifying sadness can be especially valuable in counseling or support settings, as it often suggests that a person needs empathy and reassurance, even if they are trying to keep a composed exterior.

Surprise: Surprise is evident when both eyebrows rise high, creating horizontal wrinkles across the forehead. The eyes open wide, exposing the sclera above and below the iris, and the mouth may open. Surprise is a sudden response to unexpected information. It's a transient expression that can shift quickly into another emotion, such as fear or happiness. Detecting surprise can reveal someone's initial, unfiltered response before they have a chance to mask it.

Contempt: Contempt is unique among the micro-expressions, occurring only on one side of the face. This expression typically involves a tightened and slightly raised corner of the mouth, creating a unilateral smirk. Contempt, often a sign of superiority or disapproval, is particularly revealing in interpersonal conflicts. Recognizing contempt can be essential in negotiations or mediation, as it signals underlying resentment or lack of respect.

DETECTING AND INTERPRETING MICRO-EXPRESSIONS

Recognizing micro-expressions requires training and practice:

- *Baseline Behavior:* Understanding an individual's normal expressions is crucial.
- *Context:* The situation can provide clues to which emotions might be being suppressed.
- *Clusters:* Looking for groups of cues rather than isolated signs increases accuracy.

Detecting micro-expressions requires significant training and practice. It involves not only recognizing the expressions themselves but also understanding the context in which they occur and the individual's baseline behavior. The study and application of micro-expression recognition have been controversial. While they can provide valuable insights, particularly in high-stakes situations like security screenings or police interrogations, there are concerns about privacy and the potential for misuse or misinterpretation. Micro-expression analysis has gained attention in high-stakes scenarios, such as security screenings, police interrogations, and even customer service training. However, the approach raises ethical concerns. First, there's the risk of misinterpretation, as micro-expressions, while informative, don't reveal specific thoughts or intentions (Ekman, 2003; Ekman, 2009; Ekman & Friesen, 1975). They indicate underlying emotions but are not definitive proof of guilt, honesty, or motives. This is particularly relevant in judicial settings, where over-reliance on micro-expressions can lead to wrongful conclusions.

THE INTERACTION BETWEEN EYE MOVEMENTS AND MICRO-EXPRESSIONS

Eye movements and micro-expressions indeed create a dynamic interaction that can provide deeper insight into a person's true emotions and thoughts. While both eye movements and micro-expressions offer individual clues to what someone might be feeling or thinking, they can be especially revealing when observed together. This coordination can sometimes expose subtle, concealed emotions or reveal signs of internal conflict (Ambady *et al.*, 2002; Senna, 2024). Here is a breakdown of how these elements interact and what this interplay can reveal:

Rapid Eye Movements Preceding or Accompanying Micro-Expressions

- **Precursor to Emotion**: Rapid eye movements often precede or accompany micro-expressions, serving as a prelude to an emotional response. For instance, a person might dart their eyes around quickly when feeling uncertain or before displaying a fleeting micro-expression of fear or surprise. This initial reaction often signals that the person is quickly assessing their surroundings, potentially indicating nervousness or searching for a way to mask their genuine reaction (Senna, 2024).
- **Shift in Focus and Attention**: The direction of someone's gaze can also offer context to a micro-expression. For example, when someone is surprised, their gaze might instinctively shift to the source of surprise before their facial expression registers it. Similarly, in a high-stakes environment (such as an interview), rapid eye movements before a micro-expression of fear or concern may indicate that the person is processing information under pressure (Ambady *et al.*, 2002).

Eye Movements as Indicators of Attempted Control Over Micro-Expressions

- **Discrepancies Between Eye Movements and Facial Expressions**: People often attempt to conceal their emotions, especially in professional or socially sensitive settings. While they might successfully control their facial expressions, their eye movements can sometimes betray their underlying emotions. For instance, someone might avoid eye contact or blink more frequently when they are trying to suppress emotions like anger, discomfort, or nervousness. Similarly, if a person maintains a calm or neutral face while their eyes show rapid movement or tension, it could indicate an attempt to manage a reaction they do not wish to reveal (Ekman, 2009; Vrij, 2008).
- **Darting Eyes and Micro-Expression Suppression**: When a person consciously tries to control their facial expressions, they may compensate through excessive blinking, averted gaze, or darting eye movements. These behaviors often signal discomfort or conflict, as they suggest the person is actively working to mask

their true emotions, which might show up in split-second micro-expressions (DePaulo *et al.*, 2003).

Eyes as Central to Specific Micro-Expressions (Surprise, Fear, Happiness)

- **Surprise**: Eye widening is one of the most distinctive indicators of surprise, as it's an immediate and involuntary reaction to unexpected stimuli. When someone experiences surprise, the raised eyebrows and wide eyes are often paired with an intake of breath, which may occur too quickly for conscious masking. This expression draws attention directly to the eyes and brows, making any attempt to disguise surprise quite challenging (Ekman, 2003).
- **Fear**: Like surprise, fear also manifests primarily in the eyes, with widened eyes and raised drawn-together eyebrows. However, the emotion of fear is sustained longer than surprise and is often accompanied by heightened vigilance, reflected in rapid eye movements as the person evaluates their surroundings for threats (Ambady *et al.*, 2002). This makes fear particularly easy to spot in situations where someone is feeling exposed or anxious, despite attempts to keep a calm demeanor.
- **Happiness**: The eyes play a crucial role in distinguishing genuine happiness from a mere polite smile. In genuine happiness, the muscles around the eyes contract, creating "crow's feet" wrinkles, and the lower eyelids are pushed up (Ekman & Friesen, 1975). This involuntary engagement of the eye muscles signals authentic joy, which is difficult to fake effectively because it engages specific muscle groups tied to genuine emotional responses.

APPLICATIONS AND ETHICAL CONSIDERATIONS

Understanding eye movements and micro-expressions has applications in various fields (Allen, 2021; DePaulo *et al.*, 2003; Vrij, 2008):

Law Enforcement

Eye movements and micro-expressions can provide valuable cues for identifying deception. Law enforcement officers can use this information during interrogations or interviews to assess the credibility of a suspect or witness (Vrij, 2008). By observing nonverbal cues, investigators can better understand a witness's emotional state, which may indicate the accuracy of their recollection. This can help in gathering more reliable testimonies and constructing accurate narratives of events (DePaulo *et al.*, 2003).

Psychology

Psychologists can analyze eye movements and micro-expressions to gain insights into a person's emotional state. This understanding can assist in diagnosing mental health conditions, such as anxiety or depression, by revealing subconscious feelings that may not be verbally expressed. Researchers can study how individuals process information and respond to stimuli by examining their eye movements. This can lead to a deeper understanding of cognitive processes and contribute to cognitive psychology theories (Allen, 2021).

Business

In high-stakes negotiations, understanding eye movements and micro-expressions can provide negotiators with insights into their counterparts' emotions and intentions. This knowledge can help them adapt their strategies for more effective negotiations. Training customer service representatives to recognize micro-expressions can improve their ability to empathize with customers and respond to their needs. This can lead to better customer experience and increased satisfaction (Ekman, 2009).

Education

Teachers can utilize eye-tracking technology and micro-expression analysis to gauge student engagement during lessons. By understanding when students appear disinterested or confused, educators can adjust their teaching strategies in real time to foster better learning environments. However, ethical considerations are paramount. The power to potentially "read minds" through these cues comes with great responsibility and the risk of misuse. Observing students' nonverbal responses can also help teachers provide more targeted feedback, ensuring that students receive the support they need to grasp challenging concepts (Allen, 2021; Rayner, 1998).

CONCLUSION

Eye movements and micro-expressions provide a fascinating window into human cognition and emotion. While they offer powerful insights, it is crucial to remember that they are just one part of the complex tapestry of human communication. Accurate interpretation requires considering multiple cues, context, and individual differences. As our understanding of these subtle signals grows, so does our appreciation for the intricacy of human nonverbal communication. This detailed content provides a comprehensive exploration of eye movements and micro-expressions, covering their foundations, types, meanings, detection, and applications. As we continue to decode the subtleties of non-verbal communication, the following questions arise: How can emerging technologies further enhance our understanding of these intricate, involuntary signals and what new frontiers might they open in human interaction?

Class Activity: "Micro-expression Marathon"

"To reinforce the understanding of micro-expressions, the following class activity, 'Micro-expression Marathon,' is designed to enhance recognition skills through rapid exposure."

Duration: 45 minutes

Materials needed: Computer, projector, pre-prepared slideshow of micro-expressions

Instructions:

1. Prepare a slideshow with 30-40 images of various micro-expressions, each shown for only 0.5 seconds.
2. Provide participants with a list of basic emotions (joy, sadness, anger, fear, disgust, surprise, contempt).
3. Show the slideshow, pausing briefly after each image.
4. Participants quickly write down which emotion they believe was expressed.
5. After the slideshow, review each expression, discussing the subtle cues that indicate each emotion.
6. Have participants tally their correct answers and discuss:
   - Which expressions were easiest/hardest to identify?
   - How might this skill be useful in daily life or professional settings?

CHAPTER 3

Decoding Hand Gestures and Body Language

Abstract: Hand gestures and body language are integral components of communication, often conveying messages more powerfully than words. This chapter categorizes hand gestures into iconic, deictic, and symbolic types, explaining their specific roles in communication. It also examines body posture, focusing on how open *versus* closed stances communicate confidence, defensiveness, or vulnerability. The chapter explores the evolutionary origins of these behaviors, explaining how ancient gestures and postures continue to influence modern communication. Beyond individual gestures and postures, the chapter delves into cultural differences, shedding light on the universality and variability of these nonverbal signals across diverse contexts. Additionally, the psychological impact of body language on both the observer and the person displaying the cues is discussed. Readers will learn practical strategies to interpret and apply body language and gestures effectively in personal and professional interactions. Interactive exercises and real-life case studies offer opportunities for readers to apply these concepts in various scenarios, enhancing their communication and interpersonal relationships.

Keywords: Body language, Cultural variations, Hand gestures, Interpersonal interaction, Posture.

INTRODUCTION

Kinesics, the study of body movements, postures, and gestures, forms a crucial part of nonverbal communication. This chapter delves into the intricate world of body language, with a particular focus on hand gestures. These silent signals often convey messages more powerfully than words, revealing emotions, attitudes, and intentions that may be consciously or unconsciously expressed (Birdwhistell, 1970).

THE EVOLUTIONARY BASIS OF BODY LANGUAGE

Body language is an ancient and instinctive form of communication that predates spoken language, tracing its origins back to survival behaviors exhibited by our ancestors. Over millennia, gestures, postures, and facial expressions have evolved as essential nonverbal tools for expressing emotions and intentions and establishing social hierarchies within groups. Many of these behaviors continue to be universal, reflecting their deep evolutionary basis and importance across cultures and societies (Darwin, 1872).

Here is an in-depth look at some key body language gestures and postures and their evolutionary underpinnings, some of them also shown in Fig. (**1**) (Darwin, 1872; Ekman, 1999; Morris *et al.*, 2002; Pease & Pease, 2004).

Dominant Postures

Making Oneself Appear Larger: The act of standing tall, placing hands on hips, or widening the stance stems from ancient survival tactics, where appearing physically larger was an advantage. In the wild, animals often use body size as a cue for dominance, which deters aggression and establishes hierarchy without direct conflict. For humans, these postures serve a similar purpose by asserting dominance and confidence in social or competitive situations (Darwin, 1872; Pease & Pease, 2004).

Raised Chin and Open Chest: Raising the chin exposes the neck, an instinctively vulnerable area, signaling confidence and lack of fear. An open chest, with shoulders back, also conveys strength and assurance, subtly communicating to others that the individual is unthreatened and confident (Morris *et al.*, 2002). These postures are often seen in leaders or individuals who are comfortable with their authority, and they signal a readiness to engage or lead.

Hands on Hips: This stance further amplifies body size, suggesting control or authority. Placing hands on hips draws attention to the torso, a central and protected area of the body. Historically, this posture would have made an individual look more imposing, signaling dominance to rivals or potential threats and deterring conflict (Ekman, 1999).

Submissive Gestures

Hunching Shoulders and Lowering the Head: Lowering the head and rounding the shoulders is a gesture of submission found not only in humans but also in many animals. These actions minimize physical presence, signaling that the individual poses no threat. Our ancestors might have used such postures to avoid confrontation with dominant individuals within a social group, thereby maintaining harmony and social order (Darwin, 1872; Pease & Pease, 2004). In today's interactions, people may instinctively hunch or look down when they feel intimidated, shy, or in the presence of someone they perceive as higher in social rank.

Avoiding Direct Eye Contact: In evolutionary terms, direct eye contact can be a sign of challenge or aggression. Avoiding eye contact by looking down or to the side is a common submissive behavior that diffuses tension and prevents escalation. In hierarchical groups, both human and animal, avoiding eye contact is a way to acknowledge the superior status of another and signal compliance or respect, helping to maintain social stability (Ekman, 1999; Morris *et al.*, 2002).

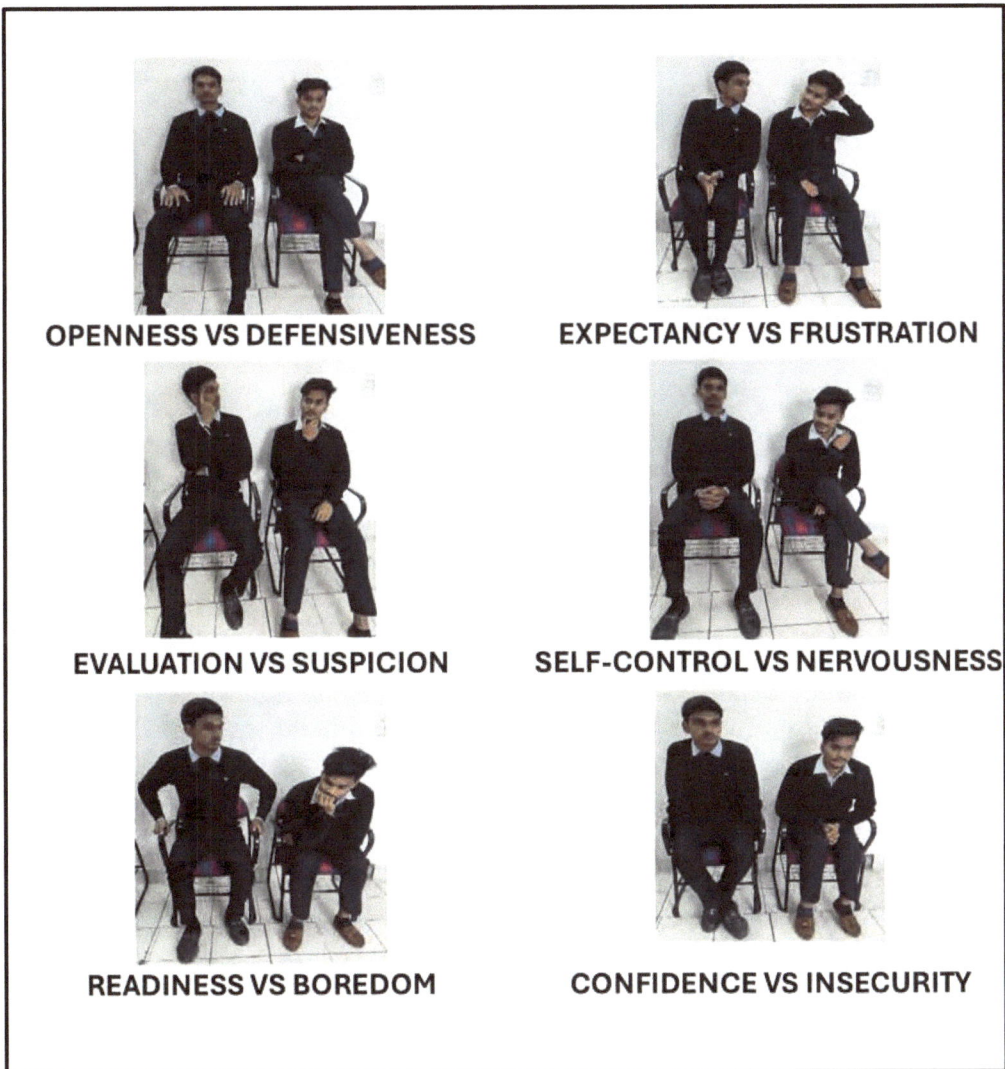

Fig. (1). Engaging Approachable Body Language. Source: Adapted from Darwin (1872); Ekman (1999); Morris *et al.* (2002); Pease & Pease (2004).

Cross-Cultural Universality of Body Language

Shared Evolutionary History: Many body language signals are remarkably consistent across different cultures, reflecting their roots in our shared evolutionary history. For example, the act of nodding in agreement or shaking the head in disagreement is nearly universal. These gestures likely emerged from basic, instinctive reactions that, over generations, became embedded in human interaction (Darwin, 1872).

Expressions of Emotion: Facial expressions, such as smiling to show friendliness or frowning to express displeasure, are other examples of universal gestures. These expressions are thought to have evolved as adaptive behaviors. A smile, for instance, signals goodwill and safety, promoting social bonding. Frowning or showing teeth can serve as an instinctive deterrent, warning others of dissatisfaction or displeasure (Ekman, 1999; Morris *et al.*, 2002).

Protective Gestures and Postures

Crossed Arms or Defensive Postures: Crossing arms over the chest is a common response to feelings of vulnerability, discomfort, or defensiveness. In evolutionary terms, this gesture protects vital organs, such as the heart and lungs, and signals a readiness to defend against threats. By closing off the body, individuals instinctively create a physical and emotional barrier to others, which remains a common reaction in uncomfortable social settings today (Pease & Pease, 2004).

Tightly Clenched Hands or Feet Pointing Toward Exits: When people feel anxious or threatened, they may clench their hands or point their feet toward an exit, even unconsciously. These behaviors stem from the fight-or-flight response, which our ancestors relied on for survival. Clenched hands prepare the body for possible action, while feet pointing toward an exit indicate readiness to leave the situation, demonstrating how body language often still mirrors primal survival instincts (Morris *et al.*, 2002).

Adaptive Social Signaling in Modern Contexts

Affiliation and Trust-Building Gestures: Touching gestures, such as handshakes or friendly pats on the back, evolved as trust-building mechanisms. Historically, extending a hand without a weapon was a gesture of peace and mutual trust, paving the way for today's handshake. Similarly, pats or hugs foster social bonding by releasing oxytocin, a hormone associated with trust and empathy. These gestures, now embedded in social etiquette, originate from primal behaviors that reinforce group cohesion (Ekman, 1999; Pease & Pease, 2004).

Mimicking or Mirroring Behavior: Mirroring the body language of others is a natural form of nonverbal communication that strengthens social bonds. Known as the "chameleon effect," this unconscious tendency to imitate another person's posture, gestures, or expressions reflects empathy and shared understanding. In evolutionary terms, mirroring served to promote cohesion and cooperation within groups, a practice that has persisted as a social bonding tool in modern society (Morris *et al.*, 2002).

Understanding this evolutionary context helps explain why certain gestures seem to be universal across cultures.

CULTURAL VARIATIONS IN BODY LANGUAGE

Cultural variations in body language are significant because they reflect each society's unique values, social norms, and communication styles. While certain nonverbal gestures, like smiling or frowning, may be universally understood, many other body language cues vary widely, making it essential to consider the cultural context to avoid misunderstandings and promote respectful communication (Axtell, 1998; Goman, 2011). (Fig. **2**).

Below is an in-depth look at several examples of body language differences across cultures, focusing on gestures, eye contact, proxemics (physical space), and touch

Gestures: Same Gesture, Different Meanings

- **Thumbs Up**: In many Western cultures, a thumbs-up is a positive gesture symbolizing approval, satisfaction, or encouragement. However, in some Middle Eastern, South American, and South Asian countries, this same gesture can be seen as vulgar or offensive, akin to showing the middle finger in Western contexts (Axtell, 1998; Pease & Pease, 2017). This cultural difference underlines how even seemingly simple gestures can be interpreted in vastly different ways depending on cultural norms.
- **The "OK" Sign (Thumb and Forefinger in a Circle)**: In the U.S. and many Western countries, the "OK" sign is a common way to indicate agreement or that everything is fine. However, in Brazil, it can be interpreted as an obscene gesture, and in some Mediterranean and Middle Eastern cultures, it may imply worthlessness or insult (Axtell, 1998; Morris, 2002). This variation illustrates the importance of being cautious with gestures in unfamiliar cultural settings.
- **Nodding and Head Shaking**: In most cultures, nodding signifies agreement, while shaking the head denotes disagreement. However, in some South Asian countries like India and Bulgaria, head movements can have different meanings. For instance, in India, a side-to-side head nod can signify agreement or

acknowledgment, which might confuse people from other regions who interpret it as a sign of negation (Axtell, 1998; Pease & Pease, 2017).

Smiling in most Western cultures Indicates someone Is happy or pleased.	In many Asian cultures, smiles can mean that the person is embarrassed.
Most Western cultures believe It is Important to maintain eye contact when conversing.	In many Asian and African cultures, it is rude to maintain eye contact, especially when speaking to someone in a senior position
In Japan, people often dose their eyes when they are listening Intently, since this blocks out other stimulations.	In most other countries, closing your eyes means you've stopped listening. Or worse, are sleeping.
Italians are known for their expressive arm gestures.	Many other cultures employ less expressive movements. Germans and British often do not move their arms at all when speaking.
In many countries, It does not matter which hand you use to give something to another person.	In the Middle East and some Asian countries, the left hand has a negative connotation and so the right hand must be used.
Finger gestures don't translate well across cultures.	In most countries, this means everything is fine. In the Arab world, this is an Insult.
In most Western cultures, this is seen as a friendly gesture.	In many Buddhist countries, the head is the home of the soul. So, It should not be touched.
In most cultures, this means that the person is concerned about getting someplace on time or is late.	In the Middle East, this is considered an Insult and Indicates that you do not see the current meeting as the best use of your time.
Most Western cultures use a handkerchief or tissue when blowing their nose to keep from spreading germs.	Asian cultures are more likely to spit or snort rather than use a soiled handkerchief that has to be kept in a pocket.

Fig. (2). Cultural variations at the global level. Source: Adapted from Argyle & Dean (1965); Axtell (1998); Goman (2011); Gunawan *et al.* (2021); Morris (2002); Patterson (2011); Pease & Pease (2017).

Eye Contact: Conveying Respect, Authority, or Disrespect

- **Direct Eye Contact**: In many Western cultures, particularly in North America and parts of Europe, maintaining eye contact is considered essential for effective communication. It is seen as a sign of attentiveness, honesty, and confidence (Argyle & Dean, 1965; Goman, 2011). However, in some Asian cultures, prolonged eye contact can be perceived as disrespectful, confrontational, or even aggressive. For instance, in Japan, direct eye contact may be avoided to show respect, particularly in hierarchical relationships, where averting one's gaze is a way to acknowledge another's seniority (Morris, 2002; Patterson, 2011).
- **Eye Contact in Middle Eastern Cultures**: In Middle Eastern countries, eye contact can vary depending on gender and context. While men may maintain strong eye contact during conversations as a show of sincerity and confidence, prolonged eye contact between men and women who are not related can be considered inappropriate or disrespectful (Axtell, 1998).
- **Latin American and Mediterranean Cultures**: In countries like Brazil, Mexico, and Italy, direct eye contact is often a sign of trust and engagement in conversation. People in these regions tend to be more comfortable with longer eye contact, viewing it as an expression of interest and respect in social interactions (Goman, 2011; Pease & Pease, 2017).

Proxemics: Preferred Distance in Conversations

- **North America and Northern Europe**: People in North American and Northern European cultures typically prefer more personal space and maintain a larger distance during conversations. Standing too close can make people uncomfortable, as personal space is highly valued. For example, in the U.S., about two to three feet is common in professional settings, which is intended to respect individual boundaries (Argyle & Dean, 1965; Gunawan *et al.*, 2021).
- **Latin America and Southern Europe**: In countries like Spain, Italy, and Mexico, people are generally more comfortable with closer proximity in social interactions. Personal space is less rigid, and stepping back during a conversation might be interpreted as standoffish or unfriendly. The closer distance reflects a more personal and expressive communication style, where physical presence is often seen as a way of building connection and trust (Morris, 2002; Patterson, 2011).
- **Middle Eastern and Asian Cultures**: In many Middle Eastern cultures, conversations between men often occur at a closer distance than in Western countries, signifying friendship and trust (Axtell, 1998). However, in Asian cultures, particularly in Japan and China, personal space is generally respected, especially in public or formal settings. Proximity with strangers is usually avoided, which is why practices like bowing have become popular in Japan as a

respectful alternative to handshakes (Gunawan *et al.*, 2021).

Touch and Physical Contact

- **Handshakes**: In Western cultures, a firm handshake is commonly seen as a sign of confidence and professionalism. However, in some Asian countries, such as China or Japan, handshakes tend to be softer and accompanied by a slight bow to show humility and respect. A forceful handshake could be seen as overly aggressive in these contexts (Goman, 2011; Axtell, 1998).
- **Hugging and Kissing**: In many Mediterranean and Latin American countries, such as Italy, Spain, and Brazil, greeting with a kiss on the cheek or a hug is a common, friendly gesture, even with people one may have just met. In contrast, North American and East Asian cultures may reserve hugging or kissing for close friends and family, with handshakes or simple verbal greetings being preferred in more formal settings (Morris, 2002; Pease & Pease, 2017).
- **Patting on the Back or Shoulder**: Patting someone on the back or shoulder is common in countries like the U.S. or Australia, where it's considered friendly or encouraging. However, in some Asian and Middle Eastern cultures, physical touch beyond handshakes can feel intrusive or inappropriate in professional or formal interactions, especially between genders (Patterson, 2011).

Facial Expressions and Smiling

- **Smiling as a Social Cue**: In many Western cultures, smiling is often used to convey friendliness, politeness, or reassurance, even in brief encounters with strangers (Patterson, 2011). However, in some Eastern European countries and East Asian cultures, people may not smile as frequently at strangers, as smiles are generally reserved for people they know well, and a smile at an unfamiliar person might be misinterpreted (Goman, 2011).
- **Expressiveness of Emotions**: In cultures like Italy, Brazil, and other Mediterranean countries, emotional expressiveness is the norm, and facial expressions are often more intense. In contrast, in cultures such as Japan or Korea, people may use neutral facial expressions to maintain harmony, respect others' boundaries, or avoid drawing attention to themselves. This difference can sometimes lead to misunderstandings when people from high-expressive cultures interact with those from more reserved societies (Morris, 2002; Pease & Pease, 2017).

The cultural variations in body language illustrate the diversity in human communication and the influence of societal values and norms on nonverbal behavior. By understanding these differences, we become better equipped to interpret body language accurately, respect cultural boundaries, and foster more meaningful and respectful interactions across diverse cultures. This knowledge promotes empathy and enriches our ability to connect with others globally.

HAND GESTURES: SILENT VOCABULARY

Hand gestures are a powerful and versatile aspect of nonverbal communication, functioning as a "silent vocabulary" that can convey a wide range of messages across cultures, even when words are not used (Ekman & Friesen, 1969; Kendon, 2004). Hand gestures can replace or enhance spoken language, clarify complex ideas, and express emotions. Although some gestures are universally recognized, many have different meanings in various cultures, highlighting the need for cultural awareness to avoid miscommunication. Here is a breakdown of the significance, versatility, and cultural variations in hand gestures (Fig. **3**).

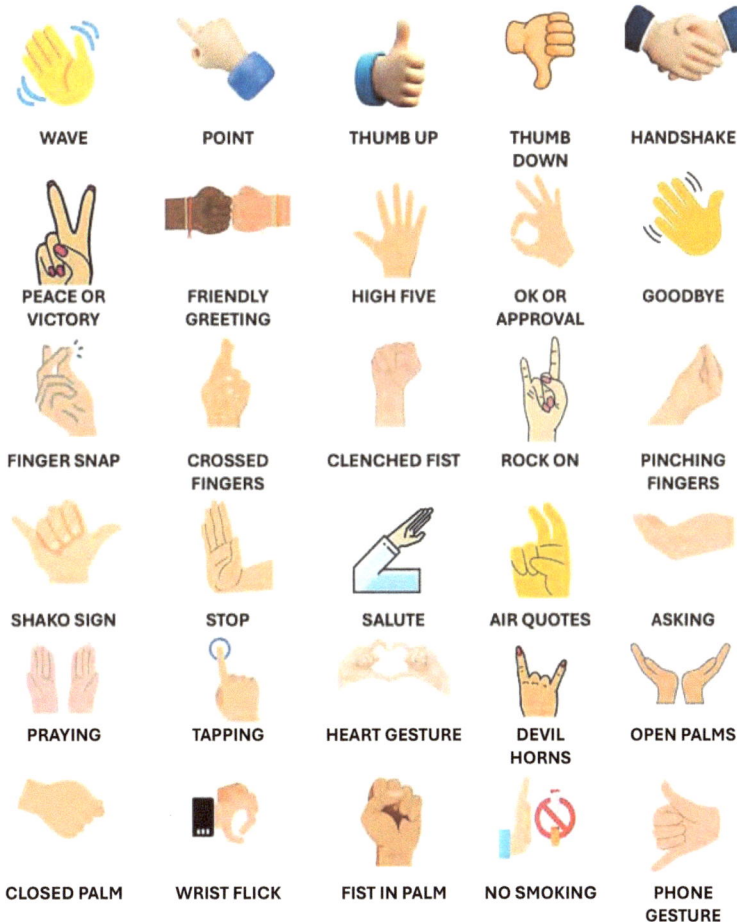

Fig. (3). Versatility and cultural variations in hand gestures . Source: Adapted from Axtell (1998); Ekman & Friesen (1969); Kendon (2004); Pease & Pease (2004).

The Role and Types of Hand Gestures in Communication

Hand gestures often accompany speech, providing emphasis, rhythm, or additional clarity to what is being said. For instance, pointing gestures can direct attention, while gestures like "air quotes" clarify sarcasm or irony. Substituting for spoken words in situations where speech is impractical or impossible, hand gestures serve as substitutes. Common examples include thumbs up for agreement, waving for greeting, or signaling a number with fingers (Axtell, 1998; Pease & Pease, 2004). Gestures can express emotions and attitudes without a single word. For instance, clenching fists often show frustration, while open palms signify honesty or openness. These emotional gestures add depth to communication and are often recognized intuitively by people across different backgrounds (Matsumoto & Hwang, 2013; Morris *et al.*, 2002):

Types of Common Hand Gestures and Their Meanings

- **Thumbs Up**: Typically used in Western cultures to indicate approval or agreement, a thumb-up has a positive connotation. However, in some parts of the Middle East, South Asia, and parts of South America, it can be offensive, signaling a rude or even obscene gesture (Axtell, 1998; Pease & Pease, 2004).
- **The OK Sign (Thumb and Forefinger in a Circle)**: In the U.S., this gesture usually signifies that something is acceptable or "okay." In contrast, it can have negative connotations in places like Brazil, where it is seen as an offensive gesture, or in some parts of Europe, where it may imply worthlessness (Ekman & Friesen, 1969; Axtell, 1998).
- **The Peace Sign (Index and Middle Finger Raised)**: The "V" sign generally symbolizes peace or victory, especially when the palm faces outward. However, in some countries like the U.K. and Australia, showing this sign with the palm facing inward can be considered rude (Pease & Pease, 2004).
- **The Wave**: A universal greeting gesture, waving can vary subtly in meaning across cultures. A palm-out wave is typically friendly and welcoming in the U.S. and Europe, while in Japan, a waving motion with the fingers (palm up) signals a beckoning gesture (Kendon, 2004). In some Asian and Latin American cultures, people may wave their hand closer to the body as an invitation to approach.
- **Finger Pointing**: Pointing with the index finger is commonly used to indicate or draw attention to something. However, in many Asian and African cultures, it can be seen as rude, and people might use the whole hand or gesture with the chin instead. In the Philippines, pointing with the lips is also common, especially in informal settings (Axtell, 1998; Pease & Pease, 2004).

The Importance of Cultural Context in Hand Gestures

- **Gesture Misinterpretations**: Many hand gestures are culturally specific, which can lead to misunderstandings when used in a different cultural context. For instance, a common gesture like the "OK" sign, while benign in some cultures, might offend or confuse people in others (Axtell, 1998).
- **High- and Low-Context Cultures**: In high-context cultures (such as those in many Asian, Middle Eastern, and Latin American countries), nonverbal communication, including gestures, plays a more significant role in conveying meaning. Meanwhile, in low-context cultures (like those in the U.S. or Northern Europe), gestures are more direct and closely tied to spoken language (Ekman & Friesen, 1969; Kendon, 2004).
- **Situational Sensitivity**: Some gestures that are acceptable in informal settings may be inappropriate in formal contexts. For example, gesturing "come here" with an index finger, common in North America, can seem disrespectful in many Asian countries, where a different hand gesture is preferred in professional or formal interactions (Pease & Pease, 2004).

Iconic, Emblematic, and Illustrative Gestures

- **Iconic Gestures**: These gestures visually represent the action or concept they describe. For example, mimicking drinking from a cup with your hand signals "drink." These gestures are often universally understood because they resemble real-world actions (Ekman & Friesen, 1969; Kendon, 2004).
- **Emblematic Gestures**: Emblems are culturally specific gestures that carry specific meanings, often without any spoken word. Examples include the thumbs-up gesture for approval or the "shaka" gesture (thumb and pinky raised) associated with Hawaiian culture to mean "hang loose" or "hello" (Axtell, 1998; Pease & Pease, 2004).
- **Illustrative Gestures**: These gestures accompany speech, often adding emphasis or helping to illustrate what is being said. An example would be tracing a large circle in the air to indicate "big" or making a chopping motion with the hand to signify decisiveness or breaking something down (Kendon, 2004).

Table **1** shows the specific cultural clashes between Western and non-Western interpretations explained as follows (Axtell, 1998; Kendon, 2004; Matsumoto & Hwang, 2013; Morris *et al.*, 2002):

Table 1. Hand Gestures in Different Cultures.

Gesture	General Meaning	U.S./ Western Culture	Asia	Middle East	Europe
Wave	Greeting/ farewell	Friendly hello or goodbye	Polite gesture in Japan	Rarely used; verbal greeting preferred	Casual in Western Europe; minimal in others
Point	Indicating direction	Common for emphasis	Considered impolite, especially in Japan	Disrespectful; whole hand often used	Rude in some areas; hand used instead
Thumbs Up	Approval/ Good	Positive, "Good job"	Can be offensive in some areas of Asia	Offensive in places like Iran	Friendly in most places; offensive in Greece
Thumbs Down	Disapproval/ Bad	Negative, means "no"	Limited usage	Often insulting	Similar to Western meaning
Peace Sign	Peace/ Goodwill	Popular for photos, "peace"	Common in photos	Not often used	Offensive if reversed (UK, Australia)
Fist Bump	Camaraderie	Friendly, casual greeting	Less common	Less common	Growing in popularity, informal greeting
High Five	Celebration	Success or agreement	Gaining popularity	Not commonly used	Growing in sports and informal settings
Okay Sign	Approval/ Okay	Positive, means "okay"	Can mean money or coins in Japan	Offensive in Turkey and Brazil	Seen as "zero" or empty in some areas
Finger Snap	Calling attention	Often seen as dismissive	Less common, may be considered rude	Little cultural significance	May be seen as rude
Crossed Fingers	Wishing luck	Represents good luck	Limited recognition	Limited recognition	Common luck gesture in most countries
Victory Sign	Victory/ Peace	Celebratory, "V for Victory"	Common in photos	Rarely used	Popular in various forms in Europe
Clenched Fist	Solidarity/ Protest	Symbol of strength/unity	Used in protests in some areas	Strong resistance symbol	Recognized in protests or rallies
Rock On Sign	Enthusiasm	Popular at concerts	Little usage, sometimes misinterpreted	Offensive in some areas like the Mediterranean	Mostly used by younger generations

(Table 1) cont.....

Gesture	General Meaning	U.S./ Western Culture	Asia	Middle East	Europe
Shaka Sign	Relaxation/ Chill	"Hang loose" sign; popular in Hawaii	Less common	Not widely recognized	Used in surfing communities
Stop Gesture	Halt or pause	Common way to ask someone to stop	Some areas may see it as abrupt	Seen as rude in some places	Seen as straightforward; can be direct
Salute	Respect or acknowledgment	Common in military contexts	Sometimes used formally	Used as a formal greeting in military contexts	Military and police contexts
Air Quotes	Sarcasm/ Irony	Used to imply sarcasm	Rarely recognized	May be misunderstood	Growing in popularity
Handshake	Greeting/ respect	Common greeting	Light handshake preferred	Often replaced with other gestures	Firm in North Europe; softer in South Europe
Waving Goodbye	Farewell	Friendly goodbye	Some countries prefer nodding	Generally uncommon	Common, although sometimes seen as informal
Pinching Fingers	Question/ Emphasis	Not common	Seen as a question or emphasis in Italy	Sometimes used to ask for patience	Strong cultural meaning in Italy; limited elsewhere

Source: Adapted from Axtell (1998); Kendon (2004); Matsumoto & Hwang (2013); Morris *et al.* (2002).

Western Culture

In Western cultures, gestures are often used for socializing, expressing emotions, and emphasizing meaning (Morris *et al.*, 2002; Axtell, 1998). For example, the **wave** is a common form of greeting or farewell. The **thumbs up** gesture is generally seen as a positive or affirmative gesture, signaling approval. **Pointing** is often used to direct attention, but it can be considered rude in other cultures (Kendon, 2004). **Peace signs** and **high fives** are also positive and celebratory gestures. However, the **okay sign** and **thumbs down** are more context-dependent; while positive in the U.S., they can be offensive in other places (Matsumoto & Hwang, 2013). Similarly, the **clenched fist** represents solidarity or protest, often seen in social movements. **Air quotes** are used to indicate sarcasm or irony, especially in informal settings (Pease & Pease, 2004).

Asian Culture

In many Asian cultures, gestures are less commonly used for casual communication, and much emphasis is placed on respect and formality (Kendon,

2004; Matsumoto & Hwang, 2013). The **wave** may be used but is often accompanied by a bow, particularly in countries like Japan and Korea. **Pointing** is considered impolite in countries like Japan, where the full hand is often used instead (Axtell, 1998). The **thumbs up** gesture, though common in Western culture, may have less significance in countries like China or Japan. The **peace sign** is often used in photos but may be less common as a greeting. **Fist bumps** and **high fives** are generally not traditional forms of greeting. The **okay sign** can have different meanings; for example, in Japan, it might represent money (Morris *et al.*, 2002). **Clenched fists** symbolize resistance and solidarity in protests, though they are not as frequently used in everyday communication. **Pinching fingers** is often associated with the Mediterranean and some Asian countries like Italy (Axtell, 1998).

Middle Eastern Culture

Gestures in Middle Eastern cultures are highly contextual and can sometimes have more significant meanings due to the cultural emphasis on hospitality, respect, and formality (Axtell, 1998). The **wave** is not as common as verbal greetings, and it is generally more formal. **Pointing** is considered rude and disrespectful, often avoided in favor of gestures that are more subtle (Kendon, 2004). The **thumbs-up** gesture, while positive in Western countries, is seen as offensive in parts of the Middle East and some Mediterranean regions. Similarly, the **peace sign** is negative if reversed, symbolizing insult. The **okay sign** is also offensive in some parts of the Middle East, such as Turkey (Morris *et al.*, 2002). **Fist bumps** and **high fives** are less commonly used, and the **handshake** is more traditional, although it's usually restricted to the same gender in more conservative areas. **Clenched fists** may symbolize protest, but it is seen with caution, depending on the situation (Matsumoto & Hwang, 2013).

European Culture

In European cultures, body language is often similar to Western norms but with slight variations (Axtell, 1998; Kendon, 2004).**Thumbs up** gesture is positive and widely accepted. **Pointing** is generally used for direction but can come across as rude if it is too direct or aggressive. **Peace signs** are commonly used for victory or positivity, but if reversed, they are offensive in the UK and Australia. The **high five** is widely recognized in sports and social contexts but may not be as frequent in formal situations. The **clenched fist** is recognized as a symbol of resistance or protest, especially in political movements. European cultures also use the **shaka sign** more in the context of relaxation or a laid-back attitude, especially in places like the Mediterranean (Morris *et al.*, 2002).

Mediterranean and South American Culture

In Mediterranean and South American cultures, gestures play a crucial role in everyday communication (Kendon, 2004; Matsumoto & Hwang, 2013). For example, the **pinching fingers** gesture, often associated with Italians, is used to emphasize a point or ask, "What are you talking about?" It can be playful or even argumentative, depending on the tone (Axtell, 1998). **Pointing** is more common here, though it may be accompanied by a more open hand in some countries. **Fist bumps** and **high fives** are less common but are gaining popularity in urban areas. The **thumbs up** gesture is recognized but can have negative connotations in some countries, such as in parts of South America. The **okay sign** is more neutral but can still be offensive in specific regions (Morris *et al.*, 2002).

Each culture has unique interpretations of body language and gestures, making cross-cultural communication both complex and fascinating. The meanings of these gestures can significantly differ, making it crucial to understand cultural context when communicating internationally.

Hand Gestures in Business and Professional Settings

- **Handshake Variations**: The handshake is widely accepted as a professional greeting, but the firmness, duration, and style vary culturally. In the U.S., a firm handshake conveys confidence, while in Japan, a lighter, brief handshake (or a bow) may be more appropriate (Axtell, 1998; Kendon, 2004).
- **Professional Gestures in Formal Contexts**: In many cultures, avoiding overly expressive gestures in professional settings is key to maintaining decorum. For instance, gestures that convey too much emotion or personality, like exaggerated arm movements, may be inappropriate in East Asian business settings, where restraint is valued (Matsumoto & Hwang, 2013).
- **Cultural Sensitivity to Touch**: In Middle Eastern, South Asian, and some European countries, personal boundaries are closely respected in professional contexts. Handshakes may be avoided altogether between men and women in some Middle Eastern cultures, where conservative practices guide social interactions (Axtell, 1998).

The Universal Language of Gestures and the Need for Sensitivity

- **Universally Understood Gestures**: Certain gestures, like waving to say hello, nodding, or shrugging shoulders to show uncertainty, are generally understood across cultures (Kendon, 2004; Morris *et al.*, 2002). However, even universally accepted gestures should be used thoughtfully, as subtle differences in interpretation exist.
- **Empathy and Awareness**: When interacting with people from different

cultures, observing and mirroring gestures can build rapport and show respect. Small adjustments, like using the appropriate level of gesture intensity, can facilitate better understanding and reduce the likelihood of misinterpretation (Matsumoto & Hwang, 2013).

Decoding Specific Hand Gestures

Hand gestures form a rich and complex "silent vocabulary" that adds depth to human communication. While some gestures convey similar meanings across cultures, many are deeply rooted in cultural traditions and norms, making it essential to understand the cultural context behind them. Some of the hand gestures can be decoded as follows (Axtell, 1998; Kendon, 2004; Noroozi *et al.*, 2021):

- *Open Palms:* Generally indicate honesty, openness, and submission.
- *Closed Fists:* Can signal aggression, determination, or stress.
- *Steepling Fingers:* Often associated with confidence and expertise.
- *Handwringing:* Usually indicates anxiety or worry.
- *Crossed Arms:* While often interpreted as defensive, this can also simply indicate comfort.

By learning about these variations and adapting our gestures accordingly, we can foster more meaningful, respectful, and effective cross-cultural interactions. This awareness ultimately enhances our ability to communicate beyond words and appreciate the diversity of human expression.

Body Posture and its Meanings

Body posture is a powerful nonverbal cue that conveys information about a person's feelings, attitudes, and intentions without a single spoken word. Often, posture reflects our mindset and mood, and it can influence how others perceive us. Body posture is also culturally influenced, as what may be considered polite or engaged in one culture might be misinterpreted in another. Here is a detailed look at various postures, their meanings, and the psychological signals they may send (Dael *et al.*, 2012; Hall, 1976; Mehrabian, 1972; Morris, 2002; Pease & Pease, 2004):

Open Posture

Open posture typically involves facing another person directly, uncrossing arms and legs, and leaning slightly forward or maintaining a neutral stance (Mehrabian, 1972; Pease & Pease, 2004). This posture generally signifies openness, attentiveness, and engagement. When people adopt open postures, it usually indicates that they are comfortable and willing to engage in interaction. This posture can also suggest honesty and a lack of defensiveness. In professional settings, an open posture can communicate approachability and confidence, often fostering a welcoming atmosphere in meetings, presentations, or interviews. In personal relationships, an open posture signals warmth and genuine interest in the other person (Dael *et al.*, 2012; Morris, 2002).

Closed Posture

Closed posture often involves crossing arms and legs or turning slightly away from the other person. Other signs include minimal eye contact or placing objects (like a bag or coffee cup) in front of the body (Dael *et al.*, 2012; Mehrabian, 1972). This posture can signal discomfort, defensiveness, or disinterest, depending on the context. For instance, crossed arms might subconsciously protect the individual's personal space, conveying an unwillingness to fully open up (Pease & Pease, 2004). However, a closed posture does not always mean disengagement; sometimes, people assume a closed posture for comfort or warmth. In group settings, a person sitting with crossed arms while others are open might feel insecure or out of place. In negotiations, crossing arms could imply resistance or skepticism, while in personal settings, it might indicate someone's need for space or a boundary (Morris *et al.*, 2002).

Mirroring

Mirroring is the subtle, often subconscious, imitation of another person's posture, gestures, or facial expressions. It might involve adopting a similar seated or standing position, leaning in when the other person does, or even matching their hand movements. Mirroring suggests rapport, empathy, and a strong level of connection between people (Pease & Pease, 2004). It is a psychological signal that can indicate agreement or mutual understanding. People often mirror the postures of those they feel comfortable with, which is why mirroring is frequently seen among close friends, partners, or colleagues who work well together. Mirroring is common in social or professional settings where building trust and connection is key. Sales professionals, for example, sometimes use mirroring to build rapport with clients. In relationships, mirroring can show attentiveness, understanding, and respect for the other person's emotional state (Dael *et al.*, 2012; Morris *et al.*, 2002).

Contrapposto Stance

This posture involves standing with weight shifted onto one leg, causing the hip to tilt slightly, with a relaxed upper body. The contrapposto stance is historically associated with art and sculpture, as seen in classic statues that often depict figures with a relaxed yet poised posture (Hall, 1976; Morris *et al.*, 2002). The contrapposto stance conveys a casual, confident, and approachable attitude. It's often associated with attractiveness, as the asymmetry of the stance creates a visually appealing look and an air of ease. The contrapposto stance is common in social or informal settings, such as at gatherings or when casually meeting people. It can make a person appear relaxed, composed, and more approachable. In professional settings, this stance can communicate self-assuredness, but it should be used carefully to maintain formality when needed (Mehrabian, 1972; Pease & Pease, 2004).

Forward Leaning vs. Reclining Posture

When someone leans forward, especially in a seated conversation, it indicates engagement, attentiveness, and eagerness to listen. It can also suggest enthusiasm and interest in what the other person is saying. Leaning forward slightly when speaking to someone can show that you are receptive and fully focused on the conversation. Leaning back can convey a sense of relaxation, comfort, and confidence, but it may also be interpreted as disinterest or even arrogance if not used appropriately. In informal settings, reclining can signal that the person is at ease; however, in a professional context, leaning too far back may create a perception of detachment or boredom (Dael *et al.*, 2012; Morris *et al.*, 2002; Pease & Pease, 2004).

Body posture is a complex and subtle language that plays a critical role in human communication. From open and closed stances to mirroring and contrapposto, each posture type sends distinct signals that others may interpret, consciously or subconsciously. Understanding these signals can improve interpersonal interactions, allowing us to gauge engagement, receptiveness, and rapport. Whether in professional or personal settings, posture communicates confidence, respect, and openness—or the lack thereof—highlighting its importance in effective nonverbal communication.

Proxemics: The Language of Space

Proxemics, or the use of space in communication, is a critical nonverbal aspect that shapes how we relate to others, perceive social boundaries, and respond emotionally in various interactions. This concept, developed by anthropologist Edward T. Hall, divides spatial usage into distinct zones—intimate, personal, social, and public—each of which has different meanings and purposes (Argyle & Dean, 1965; Gunawan *et al.*, 2021). Cultural differences, personality, context, and relationships all influence these spatial boundaries, making proxemics a dynamic and nuanced language that reveals comfort levels, social roles, and power dynamics.

Intimate Space (0-18 inches): Intimate space is reserved for close relationships, like those between family members, romantic partners, and very close friends. It is the space where the individual feels most vulnerable, as it is the closest spatial zone. In this zone, people generally feel comfortable with physical contact, such as holding hands, hugging, or whispering. Due to its very personal nature, any violation of this space by an unfamiliar person is often perceived as intrusive and can trigger feelings of discomfort or defensiveness (Argyle & Dean, 1965). In some cultures, such as Latin American and Middle Eastern cultures, close contact and smaller personal space are more common and acceptable, while in countries like the United States or Northern European cultures, individuals tend to prefer maintaining more distance, even with friends. Invading someone's intimate space without permission can lead to feelings of threat or anxiety, potentially altering the interaction by making the person appear defensive or uncomfortable. Conversely, when people welcome each other into this zone, it indicates trust, warmth, and a strong bond (Gunawan *et al.*, 2021).

Personal Space (18 inches - 4 feet): Personal space extends a bit further than intimate space and is reserved for interactions with friends, acquaintances, or colleagues (Hall, 1966). In this zone, people can engage in private conversations while maintaining a comfortable boundary. This space allows for personal conversations while preventing an overwhelming sense of closeness. Conversations in this range can be warm and engaging but are not as intimate as those that occur within the 0–18 inches zone. Different cultures have varying tolerances for personal space, which can influence how comfortable people feel during social interactions. For example, people from Mediterranean cultures may be more accustomed to close personal space, while people from Scandinavian cultures (primarily those of Sweden, Norway, and Denmark—known for distinct nonverbal communication styles rooted in their cultural values, including egalitarianism, modesty, and respect for personal space) may feel uneasy if others enter their personal space too closely (Gunawan *et al.*, 2021). Invading someone's personal space can disrupt the flow of conversation, as it may lead the individual to physically back away or mentally disengage. It can also increase stress if it feels like the other person is overly familiar or violating social norms (Argyle & Dean, 1965).

Social Space (4-12 feet): Social space is appropriate for interactions with colleagues, acquaintances, and people in more formal settings. It creates a professional distance that is neither too close nor too distant (Hall, 1966). This spatial zone is commonly observed in business meetings, networking events, and casual social gatherings where people maintain a comfortable distance while interacting. It allows for both personal interaction and professional formality. In places like the U.S. or the U.K., social space is widely respected in formal settings to avoid coming across as too familiar (Argyle & Dean, 1965). In some Eastern and Southern cultures, people may operate within slightly closer social spaces, especially in communal settings where interactions are more relationship-focused (Gunawan *et al.*, 2021). The social space helps to create a boundary that feels safe and neutral, allowing people to engage while still retaining a professional or polite distance. Crowding or shrinking this space might result in discomfort, causing individuals to withdraw emotionally or shift their attention elsewhere. Respecting social space in business interactions can establish mutual respect and a sense of professionalism.

Public Space (12+ feet): Public space is the distance maintained during large gatherings or public speaking events. It allows for broad communication with a larger audience without direct interaction. In public speaking, people naturally maintain a distance from their audience, which helps create a formal atmosphere where the speaker has control over space. This zone is also useful in casual scenarios, like observing someone from afar or passing by strangers. While public space usage is somewhat consistent across cultures, its application can vary based on formality and the number of people present. For instance, in Western cultures, it's common for speakers to use a podium to establish authority and formality, while in other cultures, speakers might move more freely within public space to promote a sense of community (Gunawan *et al.*, 2021). Maintaining a public distance in large gatherings helps to project authority, establish boundaries, and communicate effectively to a larger group without individual engagement. Invading this space (*e.g.*, by standing too close to the audience) may disrupt attention and create discomfort, while appropriately maintaining distance can instill confidence in the speaker's authority.

Proxemics are a foundational part of nonverbal communication, influencing how people perceive and interact with each other. Understanding spatial zones, cultural norms, and contextual cues in proxemics helps us interpret boundaries more accurately, enhancing our interpersonal skills and sensitivity to others' comfort. The nuanced use of space not only maintains harmony in social and professional settings but also helps individuals navigate complex cultural differences, allowing for more empathetic and effective communication.

FACIAL EXPRESSIONS AND HEAD MOVEMENTS

Broader facial expressions and head movements are powerful nonverbal signals that can convey a range of emotions and intentions. Unlike micro-expressions, which are fleeting and often involuntary, these expressions and movements are more sustained, giving observers clear insights into a person's feelings or responses. Understanding these expressions allows for deeper and more accurate communication, enhancing social connections and clarifying messages (Wu *et al.*, 2013).

Genuine *vs.* Fake Smiles

As shown in Fig. (**4**), a genuine smile reflects true happiness involving both mouth and eyes. On the other hand, a fake smile is voluntary and engages only the mouth without eye involvement.

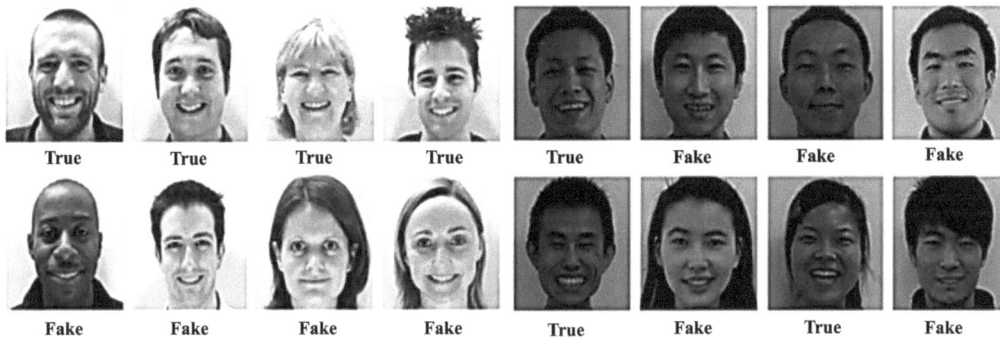

Fig. (**4**). Genuine *vs.* fake smiles. Source: Wu *et al.* (2013).

Genuine (Duchenne) Smile

Named after French neurologist Guillaume Duchenne, this smile is considered an authentic expression of happiness and involves two facial muscle groups: the zygomatic major (a facial muscle that raises the corners of the mouth) and the orbicularis oculi (a facial muscle that contracts around the eyes creating "crow's feet" at the outer corners). This full-face involvement signifies true happiness or pleasure, signaling a genuine emotional response (Wu *et al.*, 2013).

Fake Smile

Fake smiles, or "social smiles," primarily involve only the zygomatic major muscle, raising the corners of the mouth without engaging the muscles around the eyes. This smile is usually given out of politeness, social obligation, or an attempt to mask other emotions. Observers often sense the difference, as fake smiles can appear forced or insincere, affecting the overall impression of authenticity (Wu *et al.*, 2013).

Head Movements

Head movements are a powerful form of nonverbal communication, often conveying emotions, responses, or attitudes without spoken words. These movements can vary significantly across cultures and situations, providing subtle yet meaningful cues in interactions (Proske & Gandevia, 2012).

Head Nodding

A nod is widely recognized as a gesture of agreement or affirmation. In many cultures, a single or slow, deliberate nod signals understanding or approval. A sustained or emphatic nod often conveys strong agreement. Light, repetitive nodding is commonly used during conversations to show engagement and encourage the speaker to continue. This type of nodding is often accompanied by small verbal affirmations ("uh-huh," "go on") and signals active listening. While nodding generally indicates agreement in most Western cultures, there are variations. For instance, in some parts of South Asia, a nodding gesture might mean "no," and a slight head bobble might indicate agreement or acknowledgment. These nuances are critical for cross-cultural understanding to avoid misinterpretations (Argyle, 1988).

Head Shaking

A head shake generally signifies disagreement or a negative response, and in most Western and Middle Eastern cultures, it's a clear indication of "no." This movement is often instinctual and immediate, signaling a person's reaction before they vocalize it. A slow or sustained head shake can communicate disbelief, disappointment, or mild disapproval without saying a word. For instance, parents or teachers might use a slow shake of the head as a subtle reprimand or indication of disapproval, conveying their feelings without interruption. Head shaking is often accompanied by facial expressions that further clarify the meaning—such as a raised eyebrow to show disbelief or a frown to express concern. In contexts like presentations or discussions, shaking the head while listening to someone might indicate disagreement or lack of understanding, prompting further explanation from the speaker (Kendon, 2004).

Head Tilting

A slight tilt of the head, especially when accompanied by a relaxed facial expression, can signal curiosity or genuine interest in what the other person is saying. This gesture may help establish rapport, as it conveys openness and attentiveness. In contrast, a head tilt coupled with a slightly furrowed brow or pursed lips often indicates confusion or uncertainty. This expression invites clarification from the speaker, indicating that the listener is engaged but needs more information to fully understand. Interestingly, head tilting is also a behavior seen in certain animals, like dogs, which often tilt their heads to better focus on sounds (Hess *et al.*, 2009). In humans, this tilting gesture might have an evolutionary link to attentiveness or vulnerability, as it can subtly signal submission and openness, inviting others to engage more closely.

Eye Behavior Revisited

Let us do a deeper analysis of how eye movements, gaze patterns, and related behaviors reflect emotions, thoughts, intentions, or social cues (Ambady *et al.*, 2002; DePaulo *et al.*, 2003; Hess, 1975):

Eye Blocking: Eye blocking refers to actions such as covering the eyes with hands or turning the head away from what one is looking at. This behavior can indicate discomfort or distress regarding the visual stimuli or topic of discussion. For instance, during a difficult conversation about trauma or personal issues, an individual may shield their eyes to avoid confronting painful memories or emotions. Eye blocking may also occur in situations where someone feels overwhelmed, either by too much information or by an uncomfortable environment. For example, in a heated discussion or when witnessing something distressing, covering the eyes can serve as a protective mechanism, signaling a desire to disengage from the unpleasant stimulus (Ambady *et al.*, 2002; DePaulo *et al.*, 2003). Cultural norms can influence the expression of eye blocking. In some cultures, direct confrontation or the discussion of certain topics is frowned upon, leading individuals to employ eye blocking as a nonverbal cue to express their discomfort without verbally articulating it.

Eye Rubbing: Eye rubbing often occurs when someone is tired or experiencing discomfort in their eyes, such as dryness or irritation. However, it can also serve as a nonverbal signal of disbelief or a psychological response to something surprising or distressing (Hess, 1975). The act of rubbing the eyes may subconsciously serve to "unsee" an uncomfortable, shocking, or emotionally-charged situation. Eye rubbing can indicate a person's struggle to process what they are experiencing. For example, in a situation where someone hears bad news or witnesses something upsetting, rubbing their eyes may express an instinctual wish to block out the reality of the situation. Eye rubbing may also indicate fatigue during conversations or presentations, suggesting that the individual may be disengaged or struggling to focus (DePaulo *et al.*, 2003). Observers should pay attention to the context in which eye rubbing occurs, as it can reveal underlying feelings of fatigue, disbelief, or frustration.

Eyebrow Movements: Raised eyebrows can indicate surprise or interest, while furrowed brows often signal confusion or concentration. The interpretation of eyebrow movements can vary across cultures. For instance, while raised eyebrows might universally indicate surprise, in some cultures, it could also signify skepticism or questioning, particularly when paired with other nonverbal cues.

Similarly, furrowing brows in certain contexts might convey deep concern, while in others, it could be seen as a challenge or assertiveness (Hess, 1975).

BODY LANGUAGE IN VARIOUS SETTINGS

Understanding body language is essential for effective communication across different environments. The way individuals interpret and express nonverbal cues can vary significantly depending on the context, whether it be professional, personal, or public. Here is an exploration of how body language functions in these settings and its impact on communication effectiveness (Goman, 2011). Different environments call for different interpretations:

Professional Settings

Understanding body language can improve negotiation skills and leadership effectiveness:

Negotiation Skills

In professional contexts, body language plays a crucial role in negotiations. For instance, maintaining an open posture and steady eye contact can convey confidence and authority. Conversely, closed postures (*e.g.*, crossed arms) may suggest defensiveness or reluctance. Understanding these cues can help negotiators gauge the other party's readiness to compromise and adjust their approach accordingly (Pease & Pease, 2004).

Leadership Effectiveness

Leaders who are adept at reading and utilizing body language can inspire and motivate their teams more effectively. For example, using gestures that indicate openness and inclusivity can create a positive atmosphere, encouraging team members to share ideas and engage in discussions. A leader's ability to align their verbal messages with supportive nonverbal cues fosters trust and builds rapport (Goman, 2011).

Team Dynamics

Recognizing the nonverbal signals within a team can also enhance collaboration. For instance, a team member who frequently avoids eye contact might be struggling with confidence or feeling undervalued. Addressing such dynamics can improve team cohesion and productivity (Mehrabian, 1972).

Personal Relationships

Recognizing nonverbal cues can enhance emotional intimacy and conflict resolution (Harrigan *et al.*, 2005):

Emotional Intimacy

In personal relationships, nonverbal communication is pivotal in building emotional intimacy. Cues such as maintaining eye contact, physical touch, and mirroring body language can create a sense of closeness and understanding. Couples who actively engage in nonverbal expressions of affection, such as holding hands or leaning toward each other, can deepen their emotional connection (Riggio & Riggio, 2002).

Conflict Resolution

During conflicts, understanding body language can aid in de-escalating tensions. For example, recognizing signs of defensiveness (like crossed arms or avoiding eye contact) allows partners to adjust their communication style, promoting a more open dialogue. Using calming gestures and maintaining a relaxed posture can also help create a more conducive environment for conflict resolution (Graziano, 2022).

Empathy and Support

Being attuned to a partner's nonverbal cues can enhance empathetic responses. For instance, noticing a friend's slumped shoulders or averted gaze may signal distress, prompting an appropriate supportive response. This awareness fosters a stronger bond and creates a safe space for vulnerability (Riggio & Riggio, 2002).

Public Speaking

Mastering body language can significantly improve audience engagement and message delivery (Duncan, 1972):

Audience Engagement

Mastering body language is vital for effective public speaking. Presenters who use gestures to emphasize points, maintain eye contact with the audience, and vary their posture can significantly enhance audience engagement. For instance, moving around the stage confidently can convey energy and enthusiasm, drawing the audience into the presentation (Miyake & Norman, 1979).

Message Delivery

Nonverbal cues such as facial expressions and vocal tone complement the spoken message, adding depth and clarity. A speaker who smiles while delivering positive information can reinforce their message, making it more relatable. Conversely, a serious expression during a critical point can underscore the importance of the information being conveyed (Duncan, 1972).

Reading the Room

Skilled speakers can read the audience's body language to gauge their reactions and adjust their delivery in real time. For instance, if an audience appears disengaged (*e.g.*, leaning back or looking at their phones), the speaker might alter their approach, introduce a question, or incorporate a relevant story to recapture attention (Noroozi *et al.*, 2021).

Body language is a powerful component of communication that varies significantly across different settings. In professional environments, understanding nonverbal cues enhances negotiation and leadership effectiveness. In personal relationships, it fosters emotional intimacy and aids conflict resolution. For public speakers, mastering body language is essential for audience engagement and effective message delivery. By recognizing and adapting to the unique dynamics of each context, individuals can improve their communication skills and build stronger connections with others.

COMMON MISCONCEPTIONS ABOUT BODY LANGUAGE

Understanding body language is critical for effective communication, yet several misconceptions can lead to misunderstandings and misinterpretations. Addressing these popular myths is essential for fostering accurate comprehension of nonverbal cues. Table **2** shows some of the most common misconceptions about body language (Ekman, 1972; Harrigan *et al.*, 2005; Matsumoto & Hwang, 2013):

Misconceptions about body language can lead to incorrect assumptions and hinder effective communication. Understanding the nuances and complexities of nonverbal cues—such as the context in which they occur and the individual differences that influence them—is crucial for accurate interpretation. By debunking these common myths, individuals can enhance their communication skills and foster more meaningful interactions, avoiding the pitfalls of oversimplified interpretations of body language.

HOW TO IMPROVE YOUR BODY LANGUAGE READING SKILLS?

Enhancing your ability to interpret body language can significantly improve your communication skills, build stronger relationships, and foster better understanding in various contexts. Here are some practical tips to help you develop and refine your body language reading skills (Ekman, 1972; Harrigan *et al.*, 2005; Matsumoto & Hwang, 2013):

Table 2. Common Misconceptions about Body Language.

Body Language	Myth	Reality
Crossing arms always indicates defensiveness.	Crossing arms is a universal sign of defensiveness.	Crossing arms can also signify comfort, relaxation, or coldness; context is essential for interpretation.
Looking up and to the right always indicates lying.	Looking up and to the right means someone is lying.	Eye movement patterns vary by individual and culture; this direction does not universally signify deception.
Body language can be used as a foolproof lie detector.	Body language is a definitive way to detect lies.	Body language is complex and context-dependent; anxiety or nervousness may not necessarily indicate lying.

Source: Adapted from Ekman, P. (1972); Harrigan *et al.* (2005); Matsumoto & Hwang (2013).

Practice Observing People in Various Settings

- **Why it is Important**: Observing people in different environments—such as cafes, offices, or social gatherings—helps you understand how body language manifests in various contexts. Each setting can evoke different nonverbal cues based on the social dynamics at play (Knapp, 2013).
- **How to Practice**: Spend time watching interactions without being intrusive. Note the body language of individuals and groups, focusing on how they communicate their feelings and attitudes through gestures, postures, and facial expressions. Take mental or written notes to analyze later, reflecting on what these cues might signify (Pease & Pease, 2004).

Learn to Recognize Baseline Behaviors Before Interpreting Changes

- **Why it is Important**: Everyone has a unique set of baseline behaviors—typical patterns of movement, posture, and expressions that characterize them when they are relaxed or neutral. Understanding these baselines is crucial for accurately interpreting deviations that may indicate changes in emotional state or intention (Ekman, 2003).

- **How to Practice**: Pay attention to how individuals behave when they are comfortable or engaged in conversation. Observe their usual gestures, posture, and expressions. This will help you identify when someone's behavior shifts, allowing for more nuanced interpretations of their emotional states (Matsumoto & Hwang, 2013).

Consider Cultural and Individual Differences

- **Why it is Important**: Body language is not universally interpreted; cultural backgrounds, personal experiences, and social norms can significantly influence how nonverbal cues are expressed and understood. Ignoring these differences can lead to misunderstandings (Ambady *et al.*, 2002).
- **How to Practice:** Educate yourself about different cultural norms regarding body language. For example, understand that direct eye contact may be considered respectful in some cultures while seen as disrespectful in others. Be open-minded and flexible in your interpretations, considering the individual's cultural context.

Look for Clusters of Behaviors Rather Than Isolated Gestures

- **Why it is Important**: Interpreting body language should involve looking for patterns rather than relying on single gestures. A combination of nonverbal cues can provide a more accurate picture of a person's feelings and intentions (Knapp *et al.*, 2013).
- **How to Practice**: When observing someone, take note of multiple cues happening simultaneously—such as facial expressions, posture, gestures, and vocal tone. For example, if someone is crossing their arms, also consider their facial expression and overall posture. An isolated gesture might not convey the full story, while a cluster can reveal deeper insights into their emotional state.

Continuously Educate Yourself on the Latest Research in Nonverbal Communication

- **Why it is Important**: The field of nonverbal communication is constantly evolving, with ongoing research uncovering new insights into body language and its interpretations. Staying informed will enhance your understanding and ability to read nonverbal cues effectively (Matsumoto & Hwang, 2013).
- **How to Practice**: One may engage with books, articles, and online workshops dedicated to understanding body language and nonverbal communication and start with foundational materials to build a strong base. One may practice observing nonverbal cues in everyday interactions, paying attention to gestures, facial expressions, and posture in different settings. Remember, effective interpretation involves not only understanding the cues themselves but also

considering the broader context, including social, cultural, and emotional factors. For instance, the same gesture may have different meanings depending on the cultural background of the individual or the emotional tone of the situation.

Improving your body language reading skills is an ongoing process that requires observation, practice, and a willingness to learn. By following these practical tips, you can enhance your ability to interpret nonverbal cues more accurately, leading to improved communication and stronger interpersonal connections. As you develop these skills, remember that effective interpretation involves not only understanding the cues themselves but also considering the broader context in which they occur.

ETHICAL CONSIDERATIONS IN READING BODY LANGUAGE

Understanding body language is a valuable skill that can enhance communication and interpersonal relationships. However, with this power comes a responsibility to use it ethically (Allen, 2021; Johnson, 2020). Here are some key ethical considerations to keep in mind when interpreting nonverbal cues:

Respect Privacy and Avoid Making Unfounded Accusations

Body language reading involves interpreting behaviors that can be highly subjective. Misinterpretations can lead to misunderstandings and unjust assumptions about an individual's feelings or intentions. Always approach body language interpretations with caution. Avoid jumping to conclusions based solely on nonverbal cues without additional context. Recognize that what may appear as defensive body language could be influenced by external factors unrelated to the situation at hand. Respect individuals' privacy by refraining from scrutinizing their nonverbal behaviors without their consent, especially in personal or sensitive contexts (Hall, 1966).

Recognize the Limitations of Body Language Reading

Body language is not an infallible indicator of a person's thoughts or emotions. Various factors, such as individual differences, cultural backgrounds, and situational contexts, can significantly impact nonverbal communication. Maintain a healthy skepticism about your interpretations. Be aware of the complexity of human behavior and understand that body language should not be seen as a definitive source of truth. When making assessments about someone's feelings or intentions, consider seeking clarification through open and respectful dialogue rather than relying solely on nonverbal cues (Allen, 2021).

Use Your Knowledge to Improve Communication and Understanding, Not to Manipulate or Exploit Others

Ethical use of body language knowledge promotes healthy relationships and effective communication. However, there is a risk that this knowledge could be misused to manipulate or control others. Strive to use your understanding of body language to foster positive interactions, enhance empathy, and build trust. Employ your skills in a way that encourages open communication rather than using them to gain an unfair advantage or exploit vulnerabilities. Always prioritize the well-being and dignity of others in your interactions, recognizing that effective communication should be rooted in honesty and mutual respect (Johnson, 2020; Knapp *et al.*, 2013).

CONCLUSION

Decoding hand gestures and body language is both an art and a science. While certain gestures and postures have generally accepted meanings, individual differences, cultural variations, and contextual factors all play crucial roles in accurate interpretation. By developing a nuanced understanding of body language, we can enhance our ability to communicate effectively, build stronger relationships, and navigate social situations with greater ease and insight. This detailed outline provides a comprehensive exploration of hand gestures and body language.

Class Activity: "Gesture Charades"

In the "Gesture Charades" activity, participants work in small groups to convey phrases using only hand gestures and body language while others guess the phrase. The exercise helps improve nonverbal communication skills, raises awareness of cross-cultural differences in gestures, and explores how body language can enhance communication in professional settings.

Duration: 40 minutes

Materials needed: Cards with phrases or concepts, timer

Instructions:

1. Create cards with common phrases or concepts (*e.g.*, "I'm late," "I don't understand," "It's expensive").

2. Divide participants into small groups of 4-5.

3. One person from each group draws a card and has 1 minute to convey the

phrase using only hand gestures and body language.

4. Group members guess the phrase. If correct, they get a point.

5. Rotate roles within the group.

6. After 20 minutes of play, gather as a larger group to discuss:

- Which gestures were most universally understood?

- Were there any gestures that could be misinterpreted in different cultures?

CHAPTER 4

Whispers of Culture: The Silent Symphony of Nonverbal Cues

Abstract: Culture shapes how we interpret nonverbal signals, creating a "silent symphony" that guides communication in every society. This chapter explores the impact of cultural norms and values on nonverbal communication, exploring how gestures, facial expressions, and concepts of personal space vary across the globe. It introduces the concept of high-context and low-context communication cultures, providing examples that illustrate how nonverbal cues are used to convey meaning in different cultural settings. The chapter also examines the challenges of cross-cultural interactions, emphasizing the importance of cultural intelligence and adaptability. By understanding cultural variations, readers will be better equipped to navigate and interpret nonverbal cues accurately, reducing the potential for misunderstandings. The chapter concludes with practical tips for developing cultural sensitivity and leveraging nonverbal communication in multicultural environments. Case studies and cross-cultural comparisons enrich the discussion, offering insights into how global leaders and professionals adapt their communication styles to diverse audiences.

Keywords: Cross-cultural communication, Cultural intelligence, Culture, Nonverbal cues, Personal space.

INTRODUCTION

While some nonverbal expressions, such as basic emotions, are recognized universally, the interpretation and expression of most nonverbal cues are deeply influenced by cultural norms and values. This chapter explores the cultural dimensions of nonverbal communication, explaining how gestures, facial expressions, concepts of personal space, and other nonverbal signals can differ dramatically across cultures. These variations underscore the importance of understanding both universal cues and culturally specific expressions, particularly in a globalized world where cross-cultural interactions are increasingly common (Mehrabian, 1971).

Understanding these differences is essential for avoiding misunderstandings and potential offenses in cross-cultural interactions, enhancing business relationships in international contexts, improving diplomatic relations, and fostering cultural sensitivity and respect in diverse communities. Misinterpretation of nonverbal cues can lead to serious consequences, from minor social faux pas to failed business deals or even diplomatic incidents. By exploring the unique "silent symphony" of nonverbal cues within various cultural frameworks, this chapter aims to provide readers with the tools to interpret and adapt to diverse nonverbal communication styles, strengthening connections and improving understanding across cultures (Goman, 2011).

TIME PERCEPTION AS A NONVERBAL CUE

Just as gestures and facial expressions can vary, so can perceptions of time, which significantly influence social dynamics. In the area of nonverbal communication, time perception plays a significant yet often overlooked role in shaping interpersonal interactions. Different cultures interpret and express time in ways that can deeply affect social dynamics, revealing core values and social norms. Understanding these cultural variations in time perceptions, specifically the distinctions between polychronic and monochronic orientations—provides valuable insight into how people relate to one another across different contexts (Andersen, 2008; Sotak *et al.*, 2024).

Polychronic Cultures

Polychronic cultures, such as those found in Latin America, the Middle East, and parts of Africa and Asia, perceive time as fluid and flexible. In these societies, relationships take precedence over strict adherence to schedules. Time is seen as a resource to be shared rather than a commodity to be managed, leading to distinctive nonverbal cues associated with time perception (Hall, 1976):

Emphasis on Relationships

In polychronic cultures, social bonds and relationships are prioritized. For instance, arriving slightly late at a social gathering might not only be acceptable but can also be seen as a sign of respect for the relationships involved. It signals that the individual values personal connections more than mere punctuality. This perspective fosters a warm, inviting atmosphere where social interactions are prioritized over rigid schedules.

Fluid Schedules

Meetings and events may start later than scheduled, and interruptions are common as people engage in conversation. This practice emphasizes the importance of interaction itself rather than strictly adhering to time. Nonverbal cues such as relaxed body language, open posture, and frequent engagement with others reflect this cultural orientation.

Interpersonal Flexibility

In conversations, a polychronic approach allows for a more dynamic exchange. Individuals may freely switch topics, allowing for interruptions or overlap in dialogue. The nonverbal cues associated with this style often include animated gestures, proximity during discussions, and a warm, inviting demeanor.

Monochronic Cultures

Conversely, monochronic cultures, such as those prevalent in the United States, Germany, and Northern Europe, view time as a linear, structured concept. In these societies, time is treated as a finite resource that requires careful management, leading to distinct nonverbal cues that reflect this orientation (Goman, 2011):

Punctuality and Efficiency

In monochronic cultures, punctuality is not just a social expectation; it is a sign of respect and professionalism. Arriving late at a meeting or event can be perceived as a lack of reliability or consideration for others' time. Nonverbal signals in these contexts often include formal body language, such as maintaining distance, firm handshakes, and a focused demeanor that conveys seriousness and purpose.

Structured Interactions

Meetings and events are typically scheduled with specific agendas, and participants are expected to adhere to time constraints. Nonverbal cues such as checking watches, maintaining an upright posture, and limited eye contact while others speak can signify respect for the agenda and a focus on productivity.

Clear Boundaries

Monochronic cultures often establish clear boundaries around personal and professional time. For instance, individuals may not engage in social interactions during work hours or might decline social invitations if they conflict with prior commitments. Nonverbal cues reflecting this mindset include less frequent physical contact, maintaining a certain physical distance, and a preference for direct communication styles.

CULTURAL IMPLICATIONS AND MISUNDERSTANDINGS

Understanding these differences in time perception is crucial for effective cross-cultural communication. Misinterpretations can lead to misunderstandings, frustration, and even conflict (Chen, 2022; Hall, 1976; Patterson, 2001):

- **Conflicting Expectations**: A person from a monochronic culture may view a late arrival as disrespectful, while someone from a polychronic culture may see it as a natural expression of valuing relationships. This discrepancy can create tension, particularly in professional settings where punctuality is expected.
- **Adapting Communication Styles**: In multicultural interactions, being aware of time perception can help individuals adapt their communication styles. For instance, a person from a monochronic culture engaging with someone from a polychronic culture might benefit from adopting a more flexible approach, allowing for organic conversations rather than strictly adhering to agendas.
- **Building Relationships**: Conversely, those from polychronic cultures can enhance their effectiveness in monochronic contexts by demonstrating an understanding of punctuality and structure, which can foster mutual respect and collaboration.

SILENCE AS A NONVERBAL COMMUNICATION TOOL

Silence is a potent yet subtle form of nonverbal communication that often conveys more than words. Different cultures interpret and utilize silence in varied ways, with meanings that range from respect to discomfort. The cultural significance of silence can either enhance or complicate communication, particularly in cross-cultural contexts where interpretations may vary (Harrigan *et al.*, 2005; Zuckerman & Driver, 1985):

Positive Silence

In many East Asian cultures, silence is viewed as a tool of communication that fosters respect, reflection, and deeper understanding. Unlike Western cultures, where prolonged silence might be seen as awkward or uncomfortable, Eastern cultures, including Japan, China, and Korea, often value silence as an integral part of conversation:

Conveys Respect

In Japan, silence is frequently used to show respect and attentiveness. During conversations, allowing pauses after someone speaks is a nonverbal cue that demonstrates active listening and gives weight to the other person's words. The use of silence in these contexts can convey humility, as individuals take time to consider responses thoughtfully.

Encourages Reflection

Silence also serves as a moment for self-reflection and careful thought, allowing speakers to craft measured responses. This is particularly important in hierarchical or formal relationships, where silence can serve to demonstrate consideration and deliberation.

Signal Agreement or Understanding

In some East Asian contexts, silence can imply agreement or acknowledgment. Rather than verbally affirming a point, individuals might use silence as a subtle nod to understanding or alignment, which avoids unnecessary elaboration and respects the rhythm of conversation.

Negative Silence

In many Western cultures, silence is often interpreted negatively, particularly in conversational settings where active engagement is expected. Western communication styles generally favor verbal expression over silence, so prolonged quietness can be misunderstood or even perceived as hostile:

Interpreted as Disinterest or Discomfort

In cultures like those of the United States and parts of Europe, extended silence can create feelings of unease. A long pause might signal boredom, disengagement, or discomfort, prompting individuals to feel compelled to fill the gap with words, even if they have little to add. This tendency reflects the Western emphasis on continuous interaction as a sign of active participation.

May Indicate Hostility or Resistance

Silence can also be perceived as a lack of cooperation or as a passive-aggressive response. If someone goes quiet during a conversation or negotiation, it might be viewed as a sign of disagreement or defiance, even when this is not the intended message.

Can Cause Misunderstandings

When individuals from Western cultures encounter silence, they may misinterpret it as pressure to speak, potentially leading to miscommunication. This need to "fill the silence" can lead to over-explaining or hasty responses, which might not align with the intended flow of the interaction, especially if they're engaging with someone from a culture that values silence.

SILENCE IN CROSS-CULTURAL COMMUNICATION

Silence can complicate cross-cultural interactions if the underlying cultural contexts are not understood. Misinterpretations can arise when individuals from cultures with contrasting views on silence engage in conversation (Ekman & Friesen, 1971; Chen, 2022):

Risk of Misinterpreting Intentions

An East Asian individual who uses silence to show respect and thoughtfulness may be perceived as uninterested or disengaged by a Western counterpart, potentially leading to frustration on both sides. Conversely, a Western person's quick interjections to fill pauses may seem intrusive or disrespectful to an East Asian listener.

Adapting to Cultural Norms

Recognizing cultural differences in silence can help individuals navigate cross-cultural conversations with greater awareness. For example, a Western individual might consciously allow for more pauses and avoid immediately filling gaps, especially in conversations with someone from an East Asian culture. Similarly, those from cultures that value silence may benefit from understanding that Western conversational norms often encourage verbal engagement as a sign of interest.

Balancing Silence with Verbal Communication

Learning to balance silence and verbal responses based on cultural context can lead to smoother interactions and mutual respect. In a globalized world, adjusting our approach to silence can be a powerful way to foster understanding, whether in personal conversations, business meetings, or intercultural exchanges.

SYMBOLISM OF COLORS AND ATTIRE

Colors and attire function as powerful nonverbal communication tools that carry deep-rooted cultural symbolism, shaping perceptions and interactions worldwide. Each color and attire choice often reflects cultural values, norms, and traditions that influence how messages are conveyed and interpreted.

Color Symbolism

Colors hold distinct meanings across cultures, with symbolic interpretations shaped by history, tradition, and cultural significance. One color might evoke one feeling or idea in one culture, and at the same time, it can hold a contrasting meaning in another (Halo Media., 2024). Fig. (**1**) explains the psychology of colors as follows:

White Color

- **Western Societies**: In Western cultures, white is typically associated with purity, innocence, and new beginnings. It is often the traditional color for wedding dresses and other ceremonial occasions to represent virtue and sincerity (Heller, 2009).
- **East Asian Cultures**: Conversely, in many East Asian countries, white symbolizes mourning, loss, and death. White attire is commonly worn at funerals as a mark of respect for the departed. This contrast demonstrates how the same color can evoke hope and purity in one culture and grief in another, underscoring the importance of context (Heller, 2009).

Red Color

- **Chinese Culture**: Red is celebrated as a color of joy, prosperity, and good fortune. It is often used in decorations, wedding attire, and New Year festivities as a symbol of luck and vitality (Heller, 2009).
- **Western Societies**: In Western contexts, red often symbolizes danger, warning, or intense emotions like love and passion. It is common to see red used in stop signs, alarms, and emergency situations to convey urgency (Heller, 2009).

Black Color

- **Western Societies**: Black frequently represents formality, elegance, and authority. While often worn in professional settings, black is also associated with mourning and solemnity, making it a preferred color for funerals (Heller, 2009).
- **African and Indigenous Cultures**: Black can signify strength, unity, and community. In certain African traditions, black is seen as a color of connection and resilience, reflecting values that tie individuals to their ancestry (Halo Media., 2024).

RED	ORANGE	PINK
Eastern: Brides, happiness, prosperity, good fortune. **Western:** Passion, excitement, love anger, stop. **Middle East:** Danger, caution, evil	**Eastern:** Sacred, happiness, spirituality. **Western:** Harvest, autumn, warmth. **Middle East:** Mourning, loss.	**Eastern:** Marriage, feminine. **Western:** Feminine, caring, romance. **Middle East:** No color meaning
YELLOW	**WHITE**	**GREEN**
Eastern: Courage, prosperity. **Western:** Happiness, hope, summer. **Middle East:** Mourning, masculine.	**Eastern:** Mourning, unhappiness, misfortune. **Western:** Brides, medical, purity, cleanliness, holiness, surrender, peace. **Middle East:** Mourning, purity, high-ranking status.	**Eastern:** Fertility, prosperity, infidelity. **Western:** Nature, money, jealous, luck. **Middle East:** Fertility, money, holy.
BLUE	**PURPLE**	**BLACK**
Eastern: Strength, wealth, immortality, feminine. **Western:** Trust, depression, corporate, masculine, conservative. **Middle East:** Mourning, heaven, spirituality.	**Eastern:** Wealth, mobility, spirituality. **Western:** Royalty, wealth, death. **Middle East:** Wealth, loyalty.	**Eastern:** Health, knowledge, prosperity, stability. **Western:** Funerals, death, mourning. **Middle East:** Mourning, mystery, rebirth.

Fig. (1). Color psychology. Source: Adapted from Halo Media. (2024); Heller (2009).

The Role of Attire, Fashion, and Colors in Nonverbal Communication

Attire, fashion, and colors play a significant role in nonverbal communication by conveying information about a person's identity, status, and emotional state. Clothing choices can signal cultural background, profession, and even psychological traits (Pease & Pease, 2006). For example, formal attire typically conveys authority and competence, while casual clothing may suggest a more approachable and relaxed demeanor. Clothing can serve as a social signal, influencing others' perceptions and interactions. Research suggests that individuals dressed in professional attire are often perceived as more competent and authoritative than those dressed casually. Uniforms, for instance, are used in various professions to denote status, authority, and affiliation. The nuances in dress codes communicate nonverbal cues that can shape perceptions of respect, professionalism, and cultural awareness (Eicher & Ross, 2010; Halo Media., 2024; Howlett *et al.*, 2013; Sinha, 2012; Sotak *et al.*, 2024). Culturally, attire varies significantly across regions, reflecting deep-seated traditions and societal norms. For example:

- **Middle Eastern Attire:** Traditional garments like the abaya (for women) and the thobe (for men) are worn as expressions of cultural identity and adherence to values of modesty and respect, especially during religious and formal gatherings.
- **Western Business Wear:** In Western professional settings, suits and formal attire symbolize competence, authority, and professionalism. Wearing formal clothing signals preparedness and respect for workplace norms.
- **South Asian Traditional Clothing:** Garments such as sarees, kurtas, and sherwanis carry cultural and symbolic meanings. These items are often worn during festivals, weddings, and religious events, with vibrant colors and intricate patterns representing prosperity, spirituality, and community ties.
- **East Asian Attire:** In countries like Japan, the kimono and yukata represent cultural heritage, with specific patterns and colors denoting seasons, family crests, and social occasions.
- **African Traditional Wear:** Attire such as the Nigerian agbada or the Ghanaian kente cloth communicates status, heritage, and social identity. Colors and patterns are chosen for specific cultural ceremonies and convey messages of unity and pride.
- **Latin American Cultural Dress:** Traditional outfits like the Mexican charro suit or the Colombian pollera reflect historical influences and regional pride, often worn during festivals and cultural events.

Colors also carry psychological and cultural significance. Colors like red can signal dominance and passion, while blue is often associated with trust and calmness (Elliot & Maier, 2014; Halo Media., 2024). Cultural context is essential, as meanings differ globally—for instance, white represents purity in Western cultures but mourning in many Asian contexts. While this book does not delve deeply into the complexities of traditional attire across various castes and cultural groups, it acknowledges the profound impact of clothing and color in nonverbal communication across global contexts. Understanding these visual cues can improve cross-cultural interactions by fostering better communication and reducing potential misunderstandings.

Emotional Restraint *vs.* Expression in Nonverbal Communication

Cultural attitudes toward emotional expression create a unique dimension in nonverbal communication. These differences can lead to misunderstandings when people from expressive and restrained cultures interpret each other's emotional cues. Recognizing these distinctions is essential for effective intercultural interactions and helps avoid misinterpretation of sincerity, friendliness, or professionalism (Lazarus, 1991; Patterson, 2001).

Expressive Cultures

In expressive cultures, openly displaying emotions is encouraged and seen as a sign of transparency and honesty. Emotions are conveyed not only through facial expressions but also through expansive body language, voice modulation, and eye contact. This openness reflects an emphasis on personal relationships, empathy, and warmth in interactions (Lazarus, 1991; Patterson, 2001):

- **Mediterranean Cultures**: In countries like Italy, Greece, and Spain, emotions are freely shared, often with animated gestures, loud and varied vocal tones, and close physical proximity. Passion and emotional engagement are valued in social interactions, making the open display of emotions both common and socially accepted. A strong handshake, a pat on the back, or a friendly hug might be routine even with acquaintances.
- **Latin American Cultures**: In many Latin American countries, emotional expressiveness is intertwined with cultural values of warmth, friendliness, and community. People often use touch, close physical space, and direct eye contact to establish rapport and trust. In Latin American cultures, withholding emotions may be interpreted as a lack of sincerity or indifference.

Restrained Cultures

Restrained cultures, on the other hand, often view public displays of emotion as private matters that should not interfere with social harmony or professional environments. Emotional restraint reflects a focus on respect for others' boundaries, maintaining social harmony, and upholding a sense of dignity (Lazarus, 1991; Patterson, 2001):

- **Japan**: In Japan, emotional restraint is deeply embedded in social values. Maintaining a "poker face" in public settings reflects respect for others by not imposing personal emotions on them. Direct eye contact may also be minimized to show deference, particularly in professional or hierarchical relationships. While emotions are certainly felt, they're expressed more subtly, using indirect cues like slight changes in posture or voice tone.

- **Scandinavian Countries**: In countries such as Sweden, Norway, and Denmark, emotional restraint is often associated with modesty, humility, and respect for others' personal space. Interactions are generally quiet and low-key, with an emphasis on not drawing unnecessary attention. Smiling and laughter are often more subdued, and emotional highs and lows are kept private to convey a calm, reliable demeanor.

Potential Misinterpretations

The contrast between expressive and restrained cultures can lead to significant communication barriers, often resulting in misunderstandings (Patterson, 2001):

- **Expressive Cultures' View of Restrained Cultures**: Individuals from expressive cultures may interpret the reserved demeanor of restrained cultures as aloofness, disinterest, or even unfriendliness. They may feel that people in restrained cultures are "hard to read" or lack enthusiasm, which can create feelings of emotional distance.
- **Restrained Cultures' View of Expressive Cultures**: Conversely, people from restrained cultures may find expressiveness overwhelming or even unprofessional in certain settings. They may view open emotional displays as overly personal, intrusive, or exaggerated, leading them to question the sincerity or reliability of the interaction.

Bridging the Emotional Expression Gap

To overcome these differences, individuals can develop cultural sensitivity and adapt their communication styles (Ekman, 1993; Scherer & Ellgring, 2007):

- **Awareness and Adaptation**: Being aware of one's own cultural orientation towards emotional expression helps manage expectations and interpret others' behavior more accurately. For example, a Scandinavian businessperson interacting with a Brazilian counterpart might prepare to encounter a more vibrant, tactile communication style and respond with empathy and openness.
- **Contextual Sensitivity**: Understanding that emotional expression varies not only by culture but also by context (*e.g.*, professional *vs.* personal settings) enables more appropriate responses. Adapting one's level of expressiveness or restraint in different settings—such as showing more empathy and openness in informal settings and restraint in formal ones—can foster better rapport.
- **Empathy and Observation**: Paying attention to subtle nonverbal cues, such as tone of voice or slight facial changes, helps in interpreting emotions accurately, especially in restrained cultures. Empathy also encourages patience, allowing

people from different cultural backgrounds to adjust to each other's communication styles gradually.

Nonverbal Cues in Virtual Communication Across Cultures

As global teams increasingly rely on virtual communication, understanding cultural nuances in nonverbal cues becomes essential to avoid misinterpretations. Unlike in-person interactions, virtual meetings limit the visibility of certain nonverbal cues, making subtle cultural differences in online etiquette and behavior more impactful:

Camera Etiquette

In virtual settings, the use of cameras has become a point of cultural divergence, affecting perceptions of engagement and respect.

Western Cultures

In the U.S., Canada, and parts of Europe, turning on one's camera is often seen as a sign of active participation and respect for the meeting. It indicates that the participant is fully engaged and attentive. Leaving the camera off may be perceived as disinterest, lack of commitment, or distraction (Hall, 1976; Siegman & Feldstein, 1978).

East Asian and Some Middle Eastern Cultures

In contrast, participants from cultures that emphasize humility and focused listening may feel that turning the camera off demonstrates respect by concentrating solely on the speaker's words. Showing one's face could be seen as overly assertive, especially in hierarchical settings, where deference to authority is essential. It may also indicate a preference for privacy, particularly in settings that involve the home or family environment in the background (Hall, 1976; Siegman & Feldstein, 1978).

Gestural Cues in Virtual Platforms

Virtual communication presents unique challenges in interpreting gestures and expressions, especially since cues may appear differently or be completely missed through a screen (Pease & Pease, 2017):

High-Context Cultures (e.g., Japan, South Korea, and Middle Eastern Countries)

In these cultures, much of the communication relies on context, indirect cues, and implied meanings. On a virtual platform, high-context participants may rely more on pauses, vocal tone, and moments of silence rather than overt gestures. However, without the context and environmental cues that provide meaning, misunderstandings with low-context cultures can arise.

Low-Context Cultures (e.g., U.S., Germany)

In low-context cultures, communication is generally more explicit, with gestures like head nods, thumbs up, and verbal affirmations used to convey understanding and agreement. In virtual settings, this emphasis on direct gestures and verbal cues can appear overly assertive or even interruptive to participants from high-context cultures. The differences in feedback styles may leave low-context communicators feeling uncertain if they do not receive immediate, visible cues of agreement from high-context counterparts.

Navigating Virtual Nonverbal Misinterpretations

To bridge cultural gaps in virtual settings, several strategies can foster better understanding and engagement (Patterson, 2001):

- **Establishing Etiquette Norms**: Begin by setting group expectations for camera use and response styles. Allow individuals to express their preferences and comfort levels openly, creating an inclusive approach where everyone can contribute without cultural misunderstandings.
- **Encouraging Verbal Confirmation**: Since nonverbal cues may be subtle or missed in virtual communication, asking participants to verbally confirm understanding or agreement can reduce ambiguity. For instance, using phrases like "Could you let me know if that makes sense?" can prompt participants from high-context cultures to confirm without feeling pressured to adopt unfamiliar gestures.
- **Using Chat and Reaction Tools**: The chat function or reaction buttons, such as thumbs up or clap icons, can offer discreet ways to participate without interruption, which may be more comfortable for participants from restrained or high-context cultures. This approach also minimizes the risk of over-interpreting ambiguous facial expressions or body language.
- **Being Mindful of Silence**: Pauses and moments of silence can hold different meanings across cultures; in virtual settings, they often indicate processing time. High-context participants may need a few moments of silence to reflect or form

a thoughtful response. Understanding that silence is not necessarily disinteresting but rather respect for the conversation can alleviate tension and prevent misunderstandings.

Cross-Cultural Misunderstandings in Business

Nonverbal cues in business interactions are critical, yet they often differ across cultures, leading to potential misunderstandings that can influence relationship dynamics, trust, and negotiation outcomes (Chen, 2022; Ekman & Friesen, 1971):

Eye Contact in Negotiations

- **U.S. and Western Cultures**: Consistent eye contact during negotiations is valued as a sign of confidence, honesty, and engagement. For many professionals in these cultures, breaking eye contact may be interpreted as a lack of interest or even dishonesty.
- **Japanese and East Asian Cultures**: Prolonged eye contact can be seen as confrontational or aggressive. In Japan, for example, maintaining more reserved eye contact shows respect and deference. Misinterpreting this as disinterest or evasiveness could risk the trust essential for successful business interactions, especially in relationship-focused cultures.

Hand Gestures and Business Etiquette

- **Thumbs-Up Gesture**: In Western contexts, a thumb-up commonly signals approval or agreement, making it suitable for casual and professional interactions. However, in certain Middle Eastern and West African cultures, this gesture has offensive connotations, leading to unintended insults if used unthinkingly.
- **Handshake Variations**: In Western business settings, a firm handshake reflects confidence and sincerity. However, in parts of Asia and the Middle East, a softer handshake—or even avoiding handshakes between genders due to cultural norms may be preferred. In India, for instance, a "Namaste" (palms pressed together) is a common greeting that conveys respect and avoids physical contact, especially when interacting with elders or those of different genders.

Influence of Historical and Religious Contexts on Nonverbal Cues

The historical and religious contexts of cultures contribute profoundly to the nuances in nonverbal communication, affecting physical interactions, gestures, and posture in both personal and professional spheres (Sotak *et al.*, 2024):

Religious Nonverbal Practices

- **Islamic Cultures**: Many Islamic cultures observe gender-based nonverbal cues rooted in religious respect, such as avoiding physical contact with the opposite gender. For example, a slight bow or nod in greeting is preferred to avoid gestures that might be deemed inappropriate.
- **Hindu and Buddhist Cultures**: Gestures like the "Namaste" in Hindu culture or a bow in Buddhist contexts carry a spiritual element that reflects reverence. In Hindu practice, Namaste symbolizes respect for the divinity within each person, reinforcing both personal humility and acknowledgment of the other's dignity.

Historical Influence on Body Language

- **Eastern European Cultures**: Decades under Soviet influence have contributed to a more restrained public body language. Older generations often exhibit reserved gestures and interactions, a reflection of the collectivist culture that emphasized uniformity and suppressed individual expressiveness. With younger generations, particularly in post-Soviet countries, there is a blend of reserved and expressive nonverbal cues influenced by exposure to Western cultures and evolving social norms.
- **Latin American Cultures**: In Latin America, centuries of blending Indigenous, European, and African cultures have led to a highly expressive communication style, where nonverbal cues are often as powerful as spoken language. Gestures, touch, and proximity are integral to conveying warmth and trust in business and social interactions, rooted in communal values and emotional expressiveness.

The Impact of Globalization on Nonverbal Communication

Globalization has significantly influenced nonverbal communication and created new norms while also challenging traditional cultural practices. As people from different backgrounds increasingly interact in business, social, and virtual spaces, nonverbal cues have evolved, sometimes blending across cultures or adapting to global expectations (Chen, 2022; Ekman & Friesen, 1971; Sotak *et al.*, 2024): (Table **1**).

Shifts in Nonverbal Communication Due to Globalization

- **Adoption of Western Business Norms**: Western business environments typically emphasize eye contact, a firm handshake, and direct communication. These norms are becoming more common worldwide, especially in multinational corporations (Chen, 2022). For instance, many international businesspeople adopt the Western handshake over traditional local greetings, such as the Japanese bow, to align with global expectations.

- **Blending of Nonverbal Customs in Multicultural Societies**: In diverse urban centers and multicultural workplaces, nonverbal behaviors often become a mix of multiple cultural influences. For instance, in Canada or the U.K., where diverse cultural groups coexist, people may adapt their personal space preferences or hand gestures to avoid misunderstandings and foster inclusivity (Sotak *et al.*, 2024).
- **Influence of Global Media**: Movies, social media, and news platforms shape nonverbal communication by spreading recognizable gestures and expressions across cultures. For example, nodding as a sign of agreement or thumbs-up as approval has become widely recognized, although some gestures may still carry different meanings in local contexts (Ekman & Friesen, 1971).

Table 1. Common Formal and Informal Attire.

Attire	Visual Representation	Meaning
Business Formal Attire		This attire reflects a highly professional, polished look. Men typically wear full suits or sports coats with dress slacks, ties, and formal leather shoes. Women may wear tailored suits, blouses with jackets or blazers, and formal skirts or pants paired with leather-soled shoes. This style is suited for traditional corporate settings and important meetings.
Casual		This is relaxed, informal attire suitable for non-professional settings. It includes comfortable clothing like jeans, sweatshirts, T-shirts, and athletic shoes. Casual wear prioritizes comfort over formality.

(Table 1) cont.....

Attire	Visual Representation	Meaning
Business Casual		This style is a blend of professionalism and comfort, ideal for modern workplaces with a more relaxed dress code. Men can wear khakis, polo shirts, button-down shirts, or sweaters, while women may choose khakis, casual skirts, or pants with a blouse or sweater. Jackets or blazers are generally optional, making this style less formal than business wear.

Source: Adapted from Chen (2022); Ekman & Friesen (1971); Sotak *et al.* (2024).

STRATEGIES FOR EFFECTIVE CROSS-CULTURAL NONVERBAL COMMUNICATION

Develop Cultural Intelligence

Gain an understanding of the cultural backgrounds of those you frequently interact with, whether in work or social settings. Learning about specific practices, such as the significance of silence in East Asian cultures or personal space in Arab cultures, can help avoid misunderstandings (Chen, 2022).

Practice Mindfulness

Be conscious of your nonverbal behaviors, such as hand gestures, eye contact, and posture. Consider how others may perceive these gestures and what cultural associations they might have (Ekman & Friesen, 1971).

Observe and Adapt

In new environments, take time to observe the nonverbal norms. By noting how people greet each other, maintain (or avoid) eye contact, or manage personal space, you can adjust your own behavior to align with the local culture (Sotak *et al.*, 2024).

Avoid Assumptions

Recognize that nonverbal cues like smiles, handshakes, or silence may not convey the same meaning everywhere. Avoid assuming that someone's nonverbal expression reflects a universal sentiment and instead remain open to understanding its specific cultural context (Chen, 2022).

When in Doubt, ask

If a nonverbal cue is unfamiliar or ambiguous, do not hesitate to politely ask for clarification. Expressing a willingness to understand different customs shows respect and can facilitate more open communication (Sotak *et al.*, 2024).

CONCLUSION

Understanding cultural differences in nonverbal communication is essential in our interconnected world. While these differences can sometimes lead to misunderstandings, they also offer rich opportunities for learning and cultural exchange. By approaching cross-cultural interactions with curiosity, respect, and flexibility, we can bridge nonverbal divides and foster more effective and harmonious global communications. For readers, applying this knowledge means developing an awareness of one's own nonverbal signals and tuning into the subtle cues of those from other cultures. In daily life, this could involve observing body language cues when meeting international colleagues, recognizing differences in personal space during business negotiations, or adjusting eye contact in a multicultural setting. By practicing cultural sensitivity and adaptability in both business and social contexts, readers can enhance their communication skills and build stronger relationships across diverse backgrounds. This detailed outline provides a comprehensive exploration of cultural differences in nonverbal cues.

Class Activity: "Cultural Nonverbal Bingo"

The *"Cultural Nonverbal Bingo"* activity is a fun, interactive way for participants to learn about diverse nonverbal cues across cultures. As they mark recognized cues on bingo cards during scenario presentations, they gain insight into how cultural misunderstandings can arise and discuss strategies for navigating these differences.

Duration: 50 minutes

Materials needed: Pre-made bingo cards with cultural nonverbal cues, markers, presentation of cultural scenarios

Instructions:

1. Create bingo cards with various culture-specific nonverbal cues (*e.g.*, "direct eye contact," "bowing," "thumbs up gesture") and distribute cards and markers to

participants.

2. Present a series of cultural scenarios or images showcasing different nonverbal behaviors.

3. Participants mark off cues they recognize on their bingo cards.

4. The first person to get "bingo" wins that round.

5. After 2-3 rounds, discuss as a group:

- Which cultural nonverbal cues were new to participants?

- How might misunderstanding these cues lead to communication breakdowns?

- What strategies can be used to navigate intercultural nonverbal differences?

CHAPTER 5

The Psychology Behind Facial Expressions

Abstract: Facial expressions are powerful indicators of emotion, rooted in both evolution and social learning. This chapter examines the psychological mechanisms explaining how and why we express emotions through our faces, from Darwin's evolutionary perspectives to contemporary research on facial action coding systems (FACS). It discusses how emotions like happiness, sadness, anger, and fear are universally recognized, yet cultural nuances influence the interpretation and appropriateness of certain expressions. The role of mirror neurons and their impact on empathy and emotional contagion is also explored, illustrating how we subconsciously mimic and respond to others' facial cues. The chapter covers the challenges of accurately reading facial expressions, especially when people try to mask their true feelings. By understanding these dynamics, readers can develop the skills to decode facial expressions effectively, enhancing communication and emotional intelligence. Practical exercises and research-backed strategies are provided to help readers interpret facial signals in different contexts, from everyday interactions to high-stakes situations.

Keywords: Emotion, Emotional intelligence, Facial action coding, Facial expressions, Psychology.

INTRODUCTION

Facial expressions are more than mere physical movements of muscles; they are the canvas upon which our inner emotional and cognitive worlds are painted. While previous chapters have explored the physical manifestations and interpretations of facial expressions, this chapter delves deep into the psychological underpinnings that drive these expressive phenomena. We'll uncover the intricate relationship between our minds and our faces, exploring the complex interplay of cognition, emotion, and social factors that shape our expressions. Understanding the psychological mechanism behind facial expressions is crucial for anyone seeking to master the art of nonverbal communication. It provides insights not just into how to read others but also into our own emotional processes and how we present ourselves to the world. This knowledge has far-reaching implications, from improving personal relationships to enhancing professional interactions and even contributing to therapeutic practices.

One of the central psychological frameworks we'll explore is the Cognitive Appraisal Theory (Lazarus, 1991), which emphasizes how individuals assess situations and the emotions these assessments trigger. This theory helps explain how our interpretations of events lead to specific facial expressions, such as a furrowed brow in response to confusion or a smile in reaction to happiness. Additionally, Emotional Regulation (Gross, 2002) plays a significant role in shaping facial expressions. By regulating emotions, individuals can suppress or amplify certain facial expressions based on social context, which is essential for effective communication. The Facial Feedback Hypothesis (Strack *et al.*, 1988) also offers valuable insight. It posits that not only do our facial expressions reflect our emotions, but they can also influence how we feel. For instance, forcing a smile may elevate one's mood, further demonstrating the reciprocal relationship between facial expressions and emotional experiences.

Building on these psychological perspectives, Charles Darwin's seminal work, *The Expression of the Emotions in Man and Animals,* remains foundational. Darwin argued that facial expressions evolved as a universal means of communication, with specific expressions linked to innate emotional responses such as fear, anger, and happiness. His theory highlights the evolutionary significance of facial expressions and their role in human survival, laying the groundwork for much modern research in the field (Darwin, 1872).

Evolutionary Origins of Facial Expressions

Facial expressions hold significant evolutionary value, acting as a bridge for nonverbal communication long before the development of language. As Charles Darwin first explored in his 1872 work *The Expression of the Emotions in Man and Animals*, facial expressions emerged as adaptive tools that enhanced survival, social cohesion, and intra-group understanding (Kavanagh *et al.*, 2022). (Fig. **1**).

Darwin's Contributions to Understanding Facial Expressions

Darwin proposed that specific facial expressions, such as raised eyebrows in surprise, evolved because they served functional purposes—raising the eyebrows widens the eyes, which enhances the field of vision and may improve awareness of surroundings (Darwin, 1872). (Fig. **1**).

Evolutionary Functions of Facial Expressions

Survival Value

- **Fear**: Expressions of fear, such as widened eyes, helped our ancestors detect potential threats in their environment. This heightened awareness would improve readiness to flee or fight in dangerous situations (Darwin, 1872).

- **Disgust**: Expressions of disgust (*e.g.*, wrinkling the nose) helped early humans avoid ingesting spoiled food or toxic substances. This reaction likely evolved to protect against illness and enhance survival (Kavanagh *et al.*, 2022).

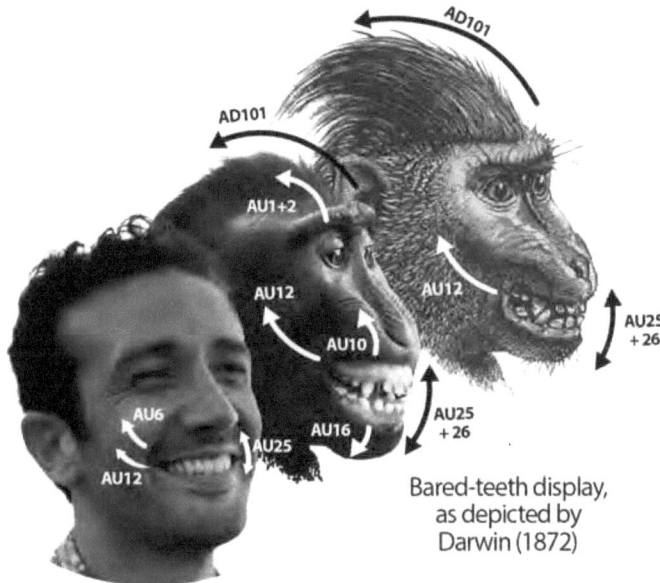

Fig. (1). Evolutionary origins of facial expressions. Source: Adapted from Darwin (1872); Kavanagh *et al.* (2022)

Social Cohesion

- **Cooperation and Group Dynamics:** Positive expressions, like smiles, play a significant role in fostering social bonds and cooperation. They signal friendliness and establish trust, which would have strengthened group ties and collaborative efforts (Kavanagh *et al.*, 2022).
- **Group Survival:** Individuals within groups who could communicate nonverbally through facial expressions would have been better equipped to coordinate and avoid conflicts, increasing the overall chances of group survival (Darwin, 1872).

Threat Display and Submission Signals

- **Threat Display (Anger)**: Expressions of anger, such as furrowed brows and tight lips, serve as a warning signal to others, indicating potential aggression. This display might dissuade others from encroaching on territory or resources, reducing direct conflict (Kavanagh *et al.*, 2022).
- **Submission Signals (Fear and Sadness)**: In tense situations, expressions of fear or sadness can signal submission and reduce the likelihood of aggression

from others. This adaptive mechanism would have been beneficial in maintaining group stability and minimizing harm (Darwin, 1872).

THE NEUROSCIENCE OF FACIAL EXPRESSIONS

Facial expressions are controlled by a complex neural network that enables us to both generate and interpret emotions. Key brain regions and mechanisms work in tandem to process and communicate emotions through facial expressions (Rout, 2023).

The Amygdala: Central to Emotional Processing

- **Role in Emotion**: The amygdala, a small, almond-shaped structure in the brain, is essential for processing emotions, particularly those related to fear and threat. This region activates in response to emotionally charged stimuli and is involved in generating expressions like fear, which serves as a survival mechanism.
- **Fear Response**: For example, when the amygdala detects a potential threat, it triggers an immediate facial response—widened eyes and raised eyebrows—that heightens awareness and enables faster reaction times.

The Motor Cortex and Facial Nerves

- **Controlling Expression**: The primary motor cortex, which governs voluntary movement, coordinates with the facial nerves to control the precise movements of facial muscles. These muscles are responsible for forming expressions such as smiles, frowns, and raised eyebrows.
- **Pathways to Facial Movement**: The motor cortex sends signals to the facial nerve, which branches out to various facial muscles, allowing us to display expressions consciously or reactively based on emotional stimuli.

Mirror Neurons and Empathy

- **Understanding and Empathy**: Mirror neurons, located in various areas of the brain, including the premotor cortex and parietal lobe, are activated when we observe someone else's facial expression. These neurons fire as if we were performing the same expression ourselves, enabling us to "mirror" and understand others' emotions.
- **Empathetic Response**: This mirroring process plays a significant role in empathy, helping us resonate with others' emotions and respond appropriately. For example, seeing someone smile can trigger a similar neural response in the observer, encouraging positive social interaction.

COGNITIVE PROCESSES BEHIND FACIAL EXPRESSIONS

The generation, modulation, and perception of facial expressions involve intricate cognitive processes, engaging different brain systems that allow us to convey a wide range of emotions and reactions (Lieberman, 2000).

Neural Pathways: Spontaneous *vs.* Voluntary Expressions

- **Spontaneous Expressions**: Emotions like surprise or fear often produce immediate, involuntary facial responses. The amygdala, integral to emotional processing, activates these spontaneous expressions, bypassing conscious control. For instance, a sudden loud noise can trigger an automatic expression of fear or startle.
- **Voluntary Expressions**: These are controlled by the motor cortex, which governs conscious muscle movement. This pathway allows us to produce intentional expressions, such as a polite smile, to align with social expectations or personal intentions.

Conscious *vs.* Unconscious Control

Facial expressions are governed by both unconscious and conscious processes, which work together to regulate how we express emotions. These processes align with the Dual-Process Theory (Evans, 2008), which distinguishes between automatic, unconscious cognitive processes and controlled, conscious ones. The dual-process theory is particularly useful in understanding how we regulate facial expressions in different contexts.

- **Dual Expression System:** Facial expressions function on two levels: spontaneous (unconscious) and controlled (conscious). Unconscious expressions are automatic and often reflect our true emotional state. For example, a sudden, spontaneous smile or furrowed brow can reveal feelings of joy or anger, even when we attempt to conceal them. These involuntary expressions provide a glimpse into our genuine emotions and can be influenced by evolutionary and social factors. On the other hand, conscious expressions are more deliberate. These expressions are the result of cognitive processing, where individuals intentionally modify their facial cues to align with social norms, cultural expectations, or situational demands. For instance, a person may consciously control their facial expression during a job interview by maintaining a neutral or pleasant demeanor, even when they feel anxious or frustrated (Dael *et al.*, 2012; Darwin, 1872; Evans, 2008).
- **Authenticity and Modulation:** The dual expression system allows for both authenticity in emotional displays and adaptability to social contexts. Automatic

(unconscious) expressions give us insight into a person's internal emotional state, while controlled (conscious) expressions enable social adaptability. For instance, an individual might consciously suppress a frown during a formal meeting to maintain professionalism, even though they may feel frustrated (Ekman, 2003).

Cognitive Appraisal: Interpreting and Reacting to Situations

- **Situational Interpretation**: Cognitive appraisal refers to how we assess and interpret situations, which directly impacts our facial expressions. The same scenario, like receiving constructive feedback, might evoke a smile in one person who sees it as a learning opportunity, while it might elicit a frown from another who perceives it as criticism (Dael *et al.*, 2012; Evans, 2008)
- **Dynamic Responses**: Our brains process and appraise situational details rapidly, adjusting expressions accordingly. These assessments often occur subconsciously, yet they deeply shape our emotional responses and outward expressions (Dael *et al.*, 2012; Evans, 2008).

Attention and Facial Expressions

- **Focus and Expression**: Attention affects not just our emotional reactions but also our facial expressions. For instance, intense concentration on a challenging task can cause facial tension, such as a furrowed brow or pursed lips, that's unrelated to any emotion (Evans, 2008).
- **Task-Oriented Expressions**: Our brains allocate resources toward tasks that require focus, leading to expressions that reflect cognitive engagement rather than emotional states. These focused expressions, while not emotional, can still convey nonverbal information to observers about our level of engagement or mental effort.

EMOTIONAL REGULATION AND FACIAL EXPRESSIONS

Facial expressions are not only a reflection of our emotions but also play a significant role in regulating those emotions. This complex interplay involves various psychological theories and practices that influence how we experience and express our feelings (Strack *et al.*, 1988; Rout, 2023). Here are key mechanisms through which facial expressions facilitate emotional regulation:

Facial Feedback Hypothesis

The facial feedback hypothesis posits that our facial expressions can affect our emotional experiences. Essentially, the way we physically express emotions can create feedback that influences our feelings. For instance, when we smile, whether out of genuine happiness or not, this act can lead to an improved mood. Research has shown that participants instructed to hold a smile, even artificially, often report feeling happier than those who maintain a neutral or frowning expression (Darwin, 1872). This phenomenon highlights the bidirectional relationship between facial expressions and emotional states.

Expressive Suppression

Expressive suppression involves consciously hiding or suppressing facial expressions as a method of emotional regulation. This strategy is often employed in social settings where displaying true emotions may be deemed inappropriate, unprofessional, or counterproductive. While this form of emotional regulation can help individuals navigate complex social interactions, its long-term use can have detrimental psychological effects (Rout, 2023). Research has consistently shown that individuals who frequently suppress their emotional expressions experience higher levels of stress, anxiety, and psychological distress (Strack *et al.*, 1988; Rout, 2023). Over time, the misalignment between felt and expressed emotions can lead to emotional fatigue, a sense of disconnection from one's true feelings, and even physical health issues, such as headaches, muscle tension, and gastrointestinal problems. Chronic suppression creates a situation where individuals are unable to process their emotions fully, often leading to a build-up of negative emotional energy. This dissonance can significantly impact mental health, contributing to burnout and depression. Additionally, studies have shown that suppression can lead to impaired emotional understanding and increased psychological strain over time. While suppression may offer short-term relief or prevent immediate conflict, its prolonged use can undermine emotional well-being and hinder the development of healthy coping mechanisms (Rout, 2023).

Cognitive Reappraisal

Cognitive reappraisal is a strategy where individuals change their interpretation of a situation to alter their emotional response. By reframing the context or meaning of an event, people can effectively shift their emotional state and, consequently, their facial expressions. For example, viewing a challenging work task as an opportunity for growth rather than a threat can help reduce anxiety. This cognitive shift often results in more relaxed and positive facial expressions, further reinforcing the new emotional state. Cognitive reappraisal is generally considered a more adaptive strategy for emotional regulation compared to expressive suppression, as it encourages a healthier emotional experience (Evans, 2008; Rout, 2023).

Emotional Labor

Emotional labor involves managing and regulating emotions to meet the emotional requirements of a job, particularly in service-oriented roles. Employees are often expected to display emotions, such as smiling, even when they don't feel them, a practice known as surface acting. While this helps in professional settings, it can lead to emotional dissonance, causing stress, burnout, and job dissatisfaction over time. Chronic emotional labor can also result in emotional exhaustion and mental health issues like anxiety and depression as employees suppress their true feelings to align with organizational expectations (Rout, 2023).

SOCIAL INFLUENCES ON FACIAL EXPRESSIONS

Facial expressions are not just individual responses to emotions; they are significantly shaped by social influences and context. Understanding these influences can enhance our grasp of interpersonal communication and emotional dynamics. Here are key social factors that impact facial expressions (Gross, 2002; Strack *et al.*, 1988):

Social Norms

Different cultures establish unwritten rules regarding appropriate emotional displays. For instance, Western cultures may encourage more open and expressive displays of happiness or excitement, while many East Asian cultures might prioritize subtlety and restraint. From a young age, individuals learn to navigate these social norms, which dictate when and how emotions can be expressed. Children observe and internalize the emotional cues of their parents and peers, leading to the development of culturally appropriate expressive behaviors (Gross, 2002). For example, in cultures that value collectivism, emotional expressions that disrupt group harmony may be frowned upon, influencing individuals to suppress their emotions.

Impression Management

People often adjust their facial expressions to align with their desired social image. This concept, known as impression management, is particularly relevant in professional and personal interactions (Gross, 2002). In work settings, individuals may suppress negative emotions and project positivity to foster a professional image, enhancing perceptions of competence and reliability. For instance, a manager might maintain a calm and friendly demeanor during stressful meetings, regardless of personal feelings. In personal relationships, individuals might exaggerate expressions of empathy or concern to connect with others emotionally. This adaptability of expression helps individuals navigate complex social landscapes and fulfill relational expectations (Rout, 2023).

Facial Mimicry

Humans have a natural tendency to unconsciously mimic the facial expressions of those around them. This mimicry serves as a form of nonverbal communication that fosters social bonds and enhances empathy (Strack *et al.*, 1988). When individuals observe someone smiling or frowning, they may involuntarily adopt similar expressions, leading to emotional contagion. For instance, during group interactions, if one person expresses joy or excitement, others may mirror that expression, contributing to a collective emotional experience. This mimicry helps create shared emotional states and strengthen group cohesion (Rout, 2023).

Power Dynamics

Social hierarchies can significantly affect how individuals express their emotions. Those in lower-power positions may feel pressured to mask negative emotions, such as frustration or disappointment, when interacting with superiors (Gross, 2022). Conversely, individuals in higher-power positions may exhibit more freedom in their emotional expressions, potentially displaying confidence or assertiveness through facial expressions. For example, a leader might openly express enthusiasm during a team meeting, reinforcing their authority and encouraging others to align with their positive outlook. Individuals lower in the social hierarchy may experience social anxiety, which can lead to less expressive behaviors (Strack *et al.*, 1988; Rout, 2023).

INDIVIDUAL DIFFERENCES IN EXPRESSIVENESS

Facial expressiveness is not uniform across individuals; rather, it is influenced by a variety of personal, psychological, and social factors. Understanding these individual differences can provide insights into how people communicate emotions and interact with others. Here are key contributors to variations in facial expressiveness (Ekman & Friesen, 1975; Gross & John, 1995; Keltner, 1995; Kring & Gordon, 1998; Riggio & Riggio, 2002; Soto *et al.*, 2011):

Personality Traits

1. **Extroversion *vs.* Introversion:** Extroverts generally display more overt facial expressions than introverts, as their comfort in social settings fosters frequent and open expressiveness. Research suggests that extroverts exhibit greater emotional reactivity in facial expressions, which enhances their ability to connect with others (Kring & Gordon, 1998). In contrast, introverts often display more reserved expressions, which can be perceived as subtle or withdrawn, affecting how others interpret their responsiveness (Riggio & Riggio, 2002).

2. **Openness:** Individuals high in openness are often more expressive and willing to show a broad range of emotions. This trait allows them to adapt easily to new social environments and may make them more approachable (Gross & John, 1995).

3. **Conscientiousness:** Conscientious individuals may consciously regulate their facial expressions to maintain professionalism. Studies indicate that those high in conscientiousness tend to exhibit controlled emotional expressions, which can be beneficial in workplace settings where emotional neutrality is valued (Matsumoto, 2006). However, this regulation may hinder spontaneous interpersonal warmth (Ekman & Friesen, 1975).

4. **Agreeableness:** Highly agreeable individuals often display positive expressions, aiming to maintain social harmony. Their expressiveness fosters trust and warmth in social interactions, enhancing relationship-building in both personal and professional settings (Soto *et al.*, 2011).

5. **Neuroticism:** Those high in neuroticism may exhibit more frequent negative expressions due to anxiety or emotional instability, which can impact their social relationships. Studies show that neurotic individuals display heightened emotional expressivity, often signaling distress or dissatisfaction, which may lead to misunderstandings (Keltner, 1995).

By understanding how these traits influence expressiveness, we gain insight into real-world communication dynamics. This awareness helps in recognizing and responding appropriately to varied emotional cues, fostering more effective and empathetic interactions.

Emotional Intelligence

In addition to personality, emotional intelligence plays a crucial role in regulating and interpreting expressions. Individuals with high emotional intelligence (EI) are typically more adept at recognizing and responding to emotional cues, both in themselves and in others. This heightened awareness allows them to display more nuanced and context-appropriate facial expressions. People with high EI are often better at regulating their emotional responses. For example, they might choose to soften their expressions in tense situations to foster a calm atmosphere or display empathy in response to others' distress (Critchley & Garfinkel, 2017).

Mental Health

Mental health conditions can significantly alter facial expressiveness. Individuals suffering from depression may exhibit reduced expression of positive emotions, often appearing flat or disengaged. This diminished expressiveness can exacerbate feelings of isolation and misunderstanding. Those with anxiety may exhibit heightened expressiveness of fear or discomfort, leading to facial cues that indicate nervousness, such as furrowed brows or pursed lips. The awareness of social scrutiny can further complicate their ability to express emotions genuinely (Dael *et al.*, 2012).

Gender Differences

While the topic remains controversial, some studies suggest that women tend to be more facially expressive than men, particularly regarding emotions like happiness and sadness. This difference is often attributed to socialization practices that encourage women to be more open with their emotions from a young age. Gender roles play a significant part in how emotions are expressed. Women may feel societal pressure to display warmth and empathy, leading to more pronounced facial expressions of care and concern. Conversely, men might suppress certain emotions due to societal expectations of stoicism, which can result in less expressive behavior, especially in public settings (Herring & Dainas, 2018).

THE DEVELOPMENT OF FACIAL EXPRESSIONS

Facial expressions are fundamental to human communication and evolve significantly throughout an individual's lifespan. This development occurs in stages, influenced by biological, social, and environmental factors. Here's an elaboration on the different stages of facial expression development, along with a diagram in Fig. (**2**), to illustrate the process (Darwin, 1872; Ekman & Friesen, 1975):

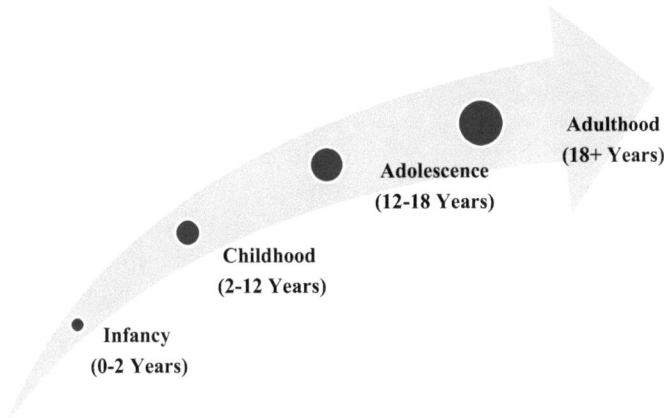

Fig. (2). Stages in facial expressions. Source: Adapted from Darwin (1872); Ekman (1993); Ekman and Friesen (1975); Hall *et al.* (2019); Hess *et al.* (2009).

Infancy (0-2 Years)

Infants begin to exhibit basic facial expressions, such as smiling and frowning, within the first few months of life (Ekman, 1993; Hess *et al.*, 2009). These expressions serve critical functions in early communication. Smiling is particularly important as it fosters attachment and bonding between the infants and caregivers. These initial expressions play a crucial role in early communication, fostering attachment and bonding between the infants and caregivers. Positive facial expressions from caregivers reinforce the infant's emotional development. Babies are also able to recognize emotional expressions in adults, which helps them learn about social interactions and emotional responses. As infants move into childhood, these early foundations of emotional recognition and expression grow in complexity, driven by interactions and environmental influences (Ekman & Friesen, 1975).

Childhood (2-12 Years)

As children grow, they become more skilled at producing and interpreting a wider range of facial expressions (Ekman, 2003; Hess *et al.*, 2009). At this stage, social interactions and experiences primarily drive this development. This development is largely facilitated by social interactions and experiences. Children learn culturally specific display rules—norms dictating how and when to express emotions. For instance, in some cultures, expressing sadness openly might be encouraged, while in others, it might be viewed as a sign of weakness (Ekman & Friesen, 1975). Interaction with peers plays a significant role in shaping emotional expressiveness, as children observe and mimic the emotional responses of others. As children move into adolescence, their emotional complexity and expression evolve with the biological and social changes of this stage (Hall *et al.*, 2019; Hess *et al.*, 2009).

Adolescence (12-18 Years)

Adolescents experience heightened emotional complexity due to hormonal changes and social pressures. This period of life involves exploring identity, which leads to more varied and nuanced facial expressions as adolescents navigate relationships and self-perception. Their facial expressions often reflect a broader range of emotions and nuances. This stage involves the exploration of identity, leading to more varied emotional expressions as adolescents navigate relationships and self-perception. Peer relationships become more prominent, influencing the way emotions are expressed (Ekman, 2009; Hess *et al.*, 2009). There may be a tendency to mask certain feelings to conform to social norms or peer expectations. With the onset of adulthood, the focus on identity and peer influence stabilizes, paving the way for a more refined approach to emotional regulation and expression.

Adulthood (18+ Years)

The basic mechanics of facial expressions stabilize in adulthood, and individuals generally express emotions consistently. However, emotional expressiveness may change as people age. As people age, they may experience changes in emotional expressiveness. Research indicates that older adults may display less intense negative emotions due to a variety of factors, including life experiences and emotional regulation strategies. Adults often develop greater emotional regulation skills, leading to more measured and controlled expressions. They may choose to express emotions more subtly in certain situations (Ekman, 1993; Hall *et al.*, 2019; Hess *et al.*, 2009). This refined approach to expression underscores the culmination of facial development across the lifespan, showcasing a lifetime of learned control and emotional adaptation.

CONTEXTUAL FACTORS AFFECTING FACIAL EXPRESSIONS

Facial expressions are not just innate reactions; they are profoundly influenced by various contextual factors that shape how we express emotions. Understanding these influences is crucial for accurately interpreting nonverbal communication in different settings (Ekman & Friesen, 1971; Hall, 1976; Patterson, 2001). Here is a detailed exploration of the key contextual factors affecting facial expressions:

Social and Cultural Context

The setting and nature of relationships significantly impact how people express emotions. In public or formal settings, such as business meetings, individuals often display more reserved facial expressions to convey professionalism. In contrast, in private settings or among close friends and family, they may feel more comfortable expressing emotions openly and showing genuine joy, humor, or other feelings (Hall, 1976; Patterson, 2001). The degree of intimacy in a relationship also affects expressiveness, as closer relationships typically encourage a more relaxed display of emotions. Cultural norms shape the expectations around emotional expressiveness. For instance, Mediterranean cultures generally embrace more passionate expressions, whereas East Asian cultures may prioritize emotional restraint and subtlety. What is viewed as a positive facial expression, like a smile, can have varied interpretations across cultures; in some settings, it conveys friendliness, while in others, it may be perceived as mockery or insincerity. Understanding these cultural differences enhances cross-cultural communication and helps prevent misunderstandings in diverse interactions (Ekman & Friesen, 1971; Hall, 1976). These combined influences provide a nuanced view of how facial expressions are shaped by both cultural background and social circumstances, enabling more adaptive and effective communication across varied social and cultural contexts.

Emotional Intensity

The intensity of the underlying emotion significantly affects the expression's intensity and duration. Strong emotions, such as joy or anger, often manifest in exaggerated facial expressions, while mild emotions may lead to subtler changes. High-intensity emotions can result in prolonged facial expressions, while lower-intensity emotions might lead to fleeting or less distinct expressions. For example, a burst of laughter may result in a wide smile that lasts longer than a quick, polite smile (Ekman & Friesen, 1971).

Conflicting Emotions

Situations that elicit conflicting emotions can lead to mixed or complex facial expressions. For example, at a farewell party, a person may feel happy for their friend but sad about their departure, resulting in a smile that is accompanied by teary eyes (Ekman & Friesen, 1971). The human face can express a range of emotions simultaneously, leading to rapid shifts in expression as a person navigates their feelings. These transitions can be difficult to read and may lead to misunderstandings, especially in cross-cultural interactions (Hall, 1976; Rout, 2023).

THE ROLE OF EMOTIONAL TEARS AND LAUGHTER IN NONVERBAL COMMUNICATION

Emotional tears and laughter are two nonverbal signals often overlooked in discussions of nonverbal communication, yet they convey significant social and emotional information. Tears, for instance, serve both physiological and social functions. Research suggests that tears can signal vulnerability and elicit empathic responses from others, enhancing social bonding (Vingerhoets, 2013). *Crying* is a powerful nonverbal cue that can express a wide range of emotions, from sadness to relief or even joy.

Similarly, *laughter* is a universal, instinctive social behavior that fosters group cohesion and signals playfulness or relief. According to Graziano (2022), laughter evolved as a defensive mechanism to signal non-threat and to promote social connection. The contagious nature of laughter underscores its role in synchronizing group dynamics and establishing rapport.

These two signals—tears and laughter—demonstrate how nonverbal communication extends beyond eye movements and gestures to include expressive behaviors that shape interpersonal interactions. The interplay of emotional tears and laughter highlights the brain's remarkable capacity to process and respond to social-emotional cues intuitively.

Facial Expressions in the Digital Age

As technology continues to evolve, so does the way we express and interpret emotions. The digital age has introduced new mediums and tools that both enhance and complicate nonverbal communication through facial expressions. Here is a closer look at how technology impacts our understanding of facial expressions (Benson & Kirby, 2019; Herring & Dainas, 2018):

Emojis and Emoticons

Emojis and emoticons have become ubiquitous in digital communication, providing a visual shorthand for expressing emotions (Fig. **3**).

Emojis can convey a wide range of feelings that might be challenging to articulate in text alone, such as happiness, sadness, sarcasm, or frustration. These symbols can enhance the emotional tone of messages, making it easier for the receiver to interpret the intended sentiment. For instance, a simple "thank you" can take on a more heartfelt meaning when paired with a smiling emoji (Benson & Kirby, 2019); Herring and Dainas, 2018). However, reliance on emojis can lead to misinterpretation. The meanings of certain emojis can vary by culture and context, potentially leading to confusion in cross-cultural communication.

Label	Emoji	Label	Emoji
"meh"		Heart Eyes	
Big Smile		Kiss	
Blush		Smile	
Crying		Tears of Joy	
Frown		Tongue Out	
Grimace		Wink	
Heart			

Fig. (3). Some common emojis. Source: Adapted from Benson & Kirby (2019); Duchowski, (2007); Hall *et al.* (2005); Herring and Dainas (2018).

Video Conferencing

The rise of remote work and virtual meetings has underscored the importance of facial expressions in communication. Participants rely heavily on visual cues to gauge engagement, agreement, and emotional reactions, as verbal cues may be less effective in a digital format. Video quality, bandwidth issues, and camera angles can distort or obscure facial expressions, making it difficult to interpret emotions accurately (Duchowski, 2007). For example, poor lighting can make it hard to see subtle expressions, while a low camera angle may emphasize different facial features, leading to misinterpretation. Cultural norms regarding facial expression may also play a role in video interactions (Hall *et al.*, 2005). Individuals from more expressive cultures might feel compelled to maintain animated facial expressions, while those from reserved cultures may exhibit less emotional display, which can be misread as disengagement.

Facial Recognition Technology

Facial recognition technology is becoming increasingly sophisticated, allowing for the analysis of facial expressions to gauge emotional states. This technology has promising applications in various fields, including marketing, security, and mental health. In marketing, companies can use facial recognition to assess customer reactions to products or advertisements in real time Duchowski, 2007). In healthcare, it can help monitor patients' emotional well-being or track responses to treatment. Despite its potential, the use of facial recognition technology raises ethical questions regarding privacy, consent, and accuracy. Misinterpretations of emotions by AI systems can lead to harmful consequences, such as incorrect profiling or stigmatization based on emotional analysis.

THERAPEUTIC APPLICATIONS OF FACIAL EXPRESSION RESEARCH

The understanding of facial expressions extends beyond social interactions, playing a crucial role in therapeutic settings. Here are some notable applications (Noroozi *et al.*, 2021; Rout, 2023):

Emotion Recognition Training

Therapies focused on improving emotion recognition are particularly beneficial for individuals with autism spectrum disorders, who may struggle to interpret facial cues. Through training programs, these individuals can learn to identify and respond to emotional expressions more effectively. Techniques such as role-playing or using technology to simulate social interactions can enhance emotional understanding and improve social skills.

Biofeedback Therapies

Biofeedback therapies utilize facial expression monitoring to help individuals gain awareness of their emotional states. By observing their expressions in real time, individuals can learn to recognize signs of stress or anxiety and develop strategies to manage their emotions more effectively. Techniques may include breathing exercises, mindfulness, or cognitive restructuring to help individuals alter their emotional responses based on their facial feedback.

Diagnostic Tools

Research into facial expression analysis is being explored as a diagnostic aid for various conditions, including depression, anxiety, and chronic pain. Clinicians may use facial cues as part of their assessment toolkit to better understand a patient's emotional state and tailor treatment plans accordingly. New technologies, such as mobile apps that analyze facial expressions and provide feedback, are emerging as potential tools for self-monitoring and enhancing mental health interventions.

CONCLUSION

The psychology of facial expressions unveils the complexity of human emotional and social life. Our faces are not mere reflections of inner states; they actively shape our emotional experiences and influence our interactions. Understanding the cognitive processes, developmental stages, and social dynamics behind expressions offers invaluable insights into human behavior and communication. This knowledge holds practical relevance across many facets of life. In daily interactions, being attuned to facial cues enhances emotional intelligence, allowing us to respond with greater empathy. In professional fields such as counseling, education, and leadership, a deeper understanding of facial expressions can foster trust, improve rapport, and aid in conflict resolution. Within personal relationships, it promotes authenticity and deeper connection, helping us navigate emotions with greater sensitivity. As we continue to explore the psychology of facial expressions, we open doors to new possibilities for personal growth, cross-cultural understanding, and mental health care. Whether in face-to-face interactions or digital communication, mastering this nonverbal language enables us to become more perceptive communicators and empathetic listeners, enriching our lives and relationships in countless ways.

Class Activity: "Emotion Mirror"

In the "Emotion Mirror" activity, participants engage in mirroring facial expressions to observe firsthand how expressions can shape emotional experiences. By reflecting on their feelings while mimicking each expression, they will explore the effects of emotional contagion and the nuances of interpreting emotions in real-life situations.

Duration: 35 Minutes

Materials needed: Computer, projector, pre-prepared slideshow of facial expressions

Instructions:

1. Prepare a slideshow with 10-15 images of distinct facial expressions.

2. Show each expression for 30 seconds, asking participants to mirror the expression.

3. After each expression, have participants write down:

- The emotion they believe the expression represents.

- How they felt while making the expression.

4. Discuss as a group:

- Did making the expression influence your emotional state?

- Were some expressions easier or harder to mimic?

- How might this relate to emotional contagion in real-life situations?

5. How do you think this exercise can help you in your own interpersonal relationships?

CHAPTER 6

The Tell-Tale Pupil: Decoding Emotions and Cognition through Pupillometry

Abstract: Pupillometry, the study of pupil size and reactivity, offers a unique window into the workings of the human mind. This chapter explores how pupil dilation reflects emotional arousal, cognitive load, and attention. By examining groundbreaking research, readers will learn how subtle changes in the pupils can indicate excitement, fear, or deep concentration. The chapter discusses the underlying neurological mechanisms, including the role of the autonomic nervous system, and how factors such as lighting and fatigue affect pupil behavior. Additionally, it addresses the practical applications of pupillometry in fields like psychology, marketing, and security. Examples illustrate how companies use pupil measurements to gauge consumer preferences or how law enforcement can assess stress responses during interrogations. Challenges in interpreting pupil data, including individual differences and the influence of external factors, are also considered. Readers will gain insights into how this seemingly minor nonverbal cue can reveal profound aspects of human cognition and emotion. Practical guidelines for observing and interpreting pupil changes are included, along with exercises to sharpen observational skills.

Keywords: Autonomic nervous system, Cognitive load, Emotion, Pupil dilation, Pupillometry.

INTRODUCTION

The eyes are often called the "windows to the soul," and for good reasons. They play a crucial role in nonverbal communication, conveying a wealth of information about our thoughts, emotions, and intentions. This chapter focuses on two key aspects of ocular communication: pupil dilation and eye contact.

Before exploring the interpretation, it is essential to understand the basic structure and function of the eye (Hess, 1975; Mathôt, 2018) (Fig. **1**):

- *Pupil:* The black center of the eye, which changes size to control light entry.
- *Iris:* The colored part of the eye that controls pupil size.
- *Sclera:* The white part of the eye.
- *Extraocular Muscles:* Control eye movement and gaze direction.

PUPILLOMETRY

Pupillometry is the scientific study of pupil size and reactivity. This fascinating field offers a unique window into the human mind, providing insights into cognitive processes and emotional states that are often beyond conscious control. The study of pupil responses dates back to the 1960s when pioneering psychologist Eckhard Hess discovered that pupil size changes not only in response to light but also to emotional and mental states (Hess, 1975). This discovery opened new avenues for understanding human psychology and cognition. Pupillometry holds a special place in nonverbal communication research because pupil responses are largely involuntary and difficult to fake, making them a potentially more reliable indicator of internal states than many other forms of nonverbal communication (Mathôt, 2018).

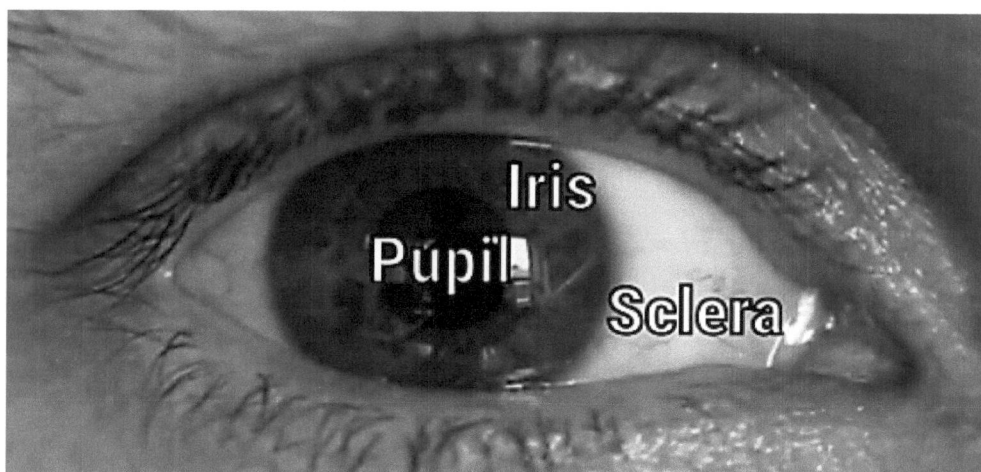

Fig. (1). Pupil, iris, and sclera. Source: Adapted from Hess (1975); Mathôt (2018).

The Physiology of Pupil Dilation

To understand the concept, we must first understand the anatomy and physiology of the pupil: The pupil is the black circle in the center of the eye, surrounded by the colored iris. It is not actually a structure itself, but rather an opening that allows light to enter the eye and reach the retina (Hess, 1975).

Pupil size is regulated by two sets of muscles within the iris: the dilator pupillae, which enlarges the pupil, and the sphincter pupillae, which constricts it. These muscles are controlled by different branches of the autonomic nervous system—the sympathetic nervous system, associated with the body's "fight or flight" response, activates the dilator pupillae, while the parasympathetic nervous system, responsible for "rest and digest" functions, controls the sphincter pupillae

(Hess, 1975; Mathôt, 2018). Several factors influence pupil size, including light levels (pupils constrict in bright light and dilate in dim light), focusing on near or distant objects, and emotional or cognitive states. Changes in pupil size occur involuntarily, reflecting underlying physiological and psychological processes (Mathôt, 2018) (Fig. **2**).

a) Constricted pupil   b) Dilated pupil

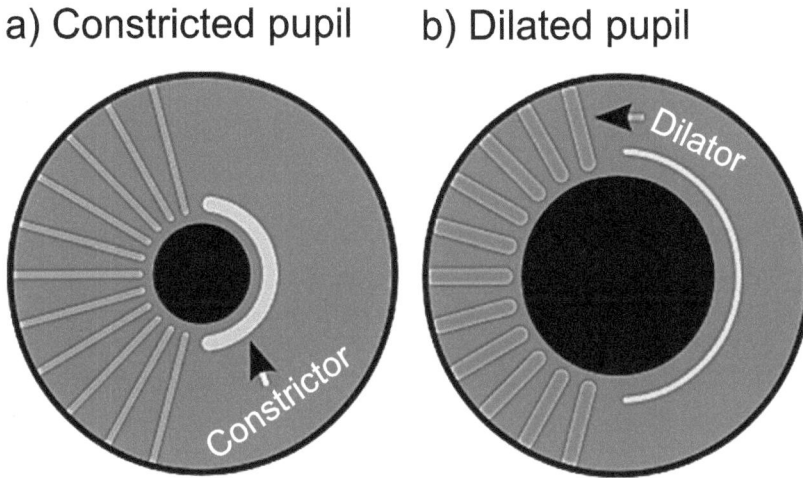

Fig. (2). Constricted and dilated pupil. Source: Adapted from Bradley *et al*. (2008); Mathôt (2018).

Psychological Factors Affecting Pupil Dilation

Pupil dilation, also known as mydriasis, is a fascinating physiological response that provides insight into various psychological states. The size of the pupil can change in response to a range of factors, including emotions, cognitive load, attraction, and decision-making processes. Below is a closer look at these factors and how they influence pupil dilation (Mathôt, 2018):

Emotional Arousal

Research indicates that both positive and negative emotional stimuli can lead to pupil dilation (Bradley *et al*., 2008). For example, viewing emotionally charged images, whether they evoke joy or fear, can trigger an increase in pupil size. This response is part of the body's autonomic nervous system activation, which prepares us for action. Stronger emotional responses tend to produce more pronounced dilation. This relationship makes pupil size a potential indicator of emotional arousal levels in various contexts, such as therapy sessions or marketing research (Hess, 1975; Mathôt, 2018). The degree of pupil dilation often correlates with emotional intensity, making it a potential indicator of arousal levels in contexts like therapy or marketing.

Cognitive Load

Pupil size increases during complex mental tasks, such as solving mathematical problems or engaging in strategic decision-making. This phenomenon is linked to the brain's demand for additional resources and cognitive effort, as pupil dilation reflects increased sympathetic nervous system activity. The extent of pupil dilation is often proportional to the difficulty of the task at hand. For instance, when individuals face more challenging or unfamiliar tasks, their pupils tend to dilate more significantly, indicating heightened mental effort and engagement (Mathôt, 2018).

Interest and Attraction

Pupils often dilate when individuals view someone or something they find attractive. This physiological response occurs unconsciously and is challenging to control, as it is rooted in the body's instinctual reactions (Hess, 1975). Research shows that this dilation occurs without conscious thought, highlighting its role as a biological indicator of interest or attraction (Mathôt, 2018). This physiological cue serves as a biological indicator of attraction, with studies showing pupil dilation when people look at attractive faces, thus influencing social interactions (Bradley *et al.*, 2008).

Decision Making

Recent research has demonstrated that changes in pupil size can serve as predictors of when a person is about to decide. As individuals weigh options, their pupils may begin to dilate in anticipation of making a choice, reflecting the cognitive processes at play. This connection between pupil size and decision-making extends to contexts involving risk and uncertainty. When individuals confront uncertain outcomes or high-stakes decisions, pupil dilation can increase as they process the available information and assess potential consequences (Kahneman & Beatty, 1966).

INTERPRETING PUPIL DILATION IN VARIOUS CONTEXTS

Given the connection between pupil dilation and psychological factors, this physiological response can be observed and interpreted in various real-world contexts. Whether in social interactions, clinical settings, marketing research, or lie detection, pupil dilation provides valuable clues to understanding emotions, decision-making processes, and even potential health issues. By applying this knowledge in these contexts, we can gain deeper insights into human behavior and physiological responses. Here is an exploration of how pupil dilation is interpreted in various social, clinical, marketing, and lie-detection scenarios (DePaulo *et al.*, 2003; Heiting, 2019).

Social Interactions

In conversations, dilated pupils can signal genuine interest or emotional engagement. When individuals are actively listening or emotionally connected to the dialogue, their pupils tend to widen. This response can indicate attentiveness and enthusiasm, enhancing the overall quality of interpersonal communication (Hess, 1975). Sustained pupil dilation while looking at someone often signifies attraction or romantic interest. This physiological response is generally unconscious, indicating a level of desire or affinity that may not be verbally expressed (Mathôt, 2018). Research has shown that individuals tend to perceive others with dilated pupils as more attractive, which can influence social dynamics.

Clinical Settings

Abnormal pupil responses, such as consistent dilation or constriction, can indicate underlying neurological issues (Heiting, 2019) (Fig. **3**). For instance, significant disparities in pupil size (anisocoria) can signal problems ranging from neurological damage to drug effects, necessitating further medical evaluation. Differences in pupil reactivity between the eyes can also serve as diagnostic indicators of health problems.

For example, a sluggish response in one pupil compared to the other may suggest potential issues such as nerve damage, increased intracranial pressure, or other medical conditions requiring attention.

Marketing and Consumer Behavior

In marketing research, pupil dilation has been used as a measure to gauge consumer interest and preference. When individuals are exposed to advertisements or products they find appealing, their pupils often dilate, reflecting heightened emotional arousal and engagement with the content. Marketers can analyze pupil responses to assess the effectiveness of their campaigns (Mathôt, 2018). Greater pupil dilation in response to specific ads can indicate stronger emotional resonance and potentially predict purchase behavior, offering valuable insights for targeting and refining marketing strategies.

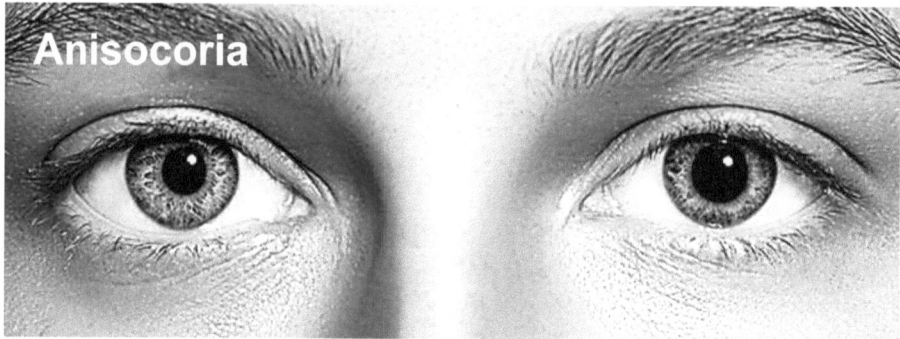

Fig. (3). Pupils with anisocoria. Source: Heiting (2019).

Lie Detection

While not a foolproof method, pupil dilation can sometimes indicate deception due to increased cognitive load or emotional arousal when an individual is lying. When someone fabricates a story or withholds the truth, their cognitive effort increases, often resulting in noticeable changes in pupil size (Mathôt, 2018).

It's essential to recognize that relying solely on pupil dilation for lie detection can lead to misinterpretations. Other factors, such as anxiety or discomfort in social situations, can also cause pupil dilation. Consequently, ethical considerations must be considered when employing physiological measures for determining truthfulness (Hess, 1975).

EYE CONTACT: BASIC CONCEPTS

Eye contact is a fundamental aspect of human interaction, serving various psychological and social functions. It involves two people looking directly into each other's eyes, playing a crucial role in regulating conversation, expressing emotions, and influencing perceptions of attitudes. Here is an exploration of the multiple dimensions of eye contact (Zuckerman & Driver, 1985):

Psychological Functions of Eye Contact

Attention and Engagement

Eye contact is a key indicator of attention in social interactions. When individuals maintain eye contact, it signifies that they are engaged and interested in the conversation. This engagement helps foster meaningful exchanges and enhances interpersonal connections. By looking at each other, conversational partners can gauge responsiveness and adjust their dialogue accordingly. Eye contact facilitates turn-taking in discussions, making interactions smoother and more dynamic (Argyle & Cook, 1976).

Emotional Communication

Eye contact can convey a wide range of emotions, from love and affection to hostility and aggression. The intensity and duration of eye contact can further amplify these emotional expressions. Prolonged eye contact can heighten emotional experiences, creating a deeper connection between individuals (Zuckerman & Driver, 1985). It can enhance feelings of empathy, compassion, and intimacy (Argyle & Cook, 1976).

Dominance and Submission

In many cultures, sustained eye contact is perceived as a display of confidence and assertiveness. It can signify an individual's authority and control within a social context. Conversely, avoiding eye contact may signal submission, respect, or difference, especially in hierarchical relationships. In certa in situations, particularly involving authority figures, individuals might avert their gaze as a sign of respect (Argyle & Cook, 1976).

Intimacy

Mutual gaze can create and enhance feelings of connection and intimacy between individuals. In romantic relationships, prolonged eye contact is often associated with deeper emotional bonds, fostering closeness and understanding (Zuckerman & Driver, 1985).

Development of Eye Contact Skills

Eye contact is one of the earliest forms of social communication between infants and caregivers. Babies naturally seek visual connection, and eye contact is essential for bonding and emotional attachment. Many individuals with ASD exhibit atypical patterns of eye contact, which can impact their social interactions. Difficulty in maintaining eye contact may affect their ability to engage with others, highlighting the importance of fostering eye contact skills in supportive environments (Argyle & Cook, 1976).

EYE CONTACT IN DIFFERENT RELATIONSHIPS AND CONVERSATIONS

Eye contact is a dynamic element of communication that varies significantly depending on the context and type of relationship. Understanding how eye contact functions in different scenarios can enhance interpersonal interactions and improve communication effectiveness.

Eye Contact Across Relationships (Duchowski, 2007)

Professional Settings

- **Conveying Confidence**: In business interactions, eye contact is often used to project confidence and authority. Maintaining eye contact while speaking can enhance the speaker's credibility and influence.
- **Establishing Rapport**: Effective eye contact helps build trust and rapport among colleagues. It signals engagement and attentiveness, making conversations more productive and collaborative.
- **Negotiations and Presentations**: During negotiations, appropriate eye contact can demonstrate sincerity and commitment. In presentations, making eye contact with the audience fosters connection and keeps their attention.

Romantic Relationships

- **Expressing Intimacy and Attraction**: In romantic contexts, prolonged eye contact can indicate attraction and emotional connection. Couples often use eye contact to convey affection and deepen their bond.
- **Nonverbal Communication of Feelings**: Eye contact serves as a nonverbal medium for expressing feelings that words may not fully capture. A lingering gaze can evoke a sense of intimacy, comfort, and mutual understanding.
- **Connection During Conflict**: During disagreements, maintaining eye contact can help individuals feel heard and validated, fostering open communication and resolution.

Parent-Child Relationships

- **Bonding and Attachment**: Eye contact is crucial for establishing emotional connections between parents and children. For infants, looking into a caregiver's eyes can reinforce feelings of security and love.
- **Emotional Regulation**: Parents often use eye contact to gauge their child's emotional state and respond accordingly. For example, making eye contact during comforting moments can help children feel supported and understood.
- **Encouraging Communication**: Parents can encourage their children to express themselves verbally and nonverbally by maintaining eye contact during conversations. This practice helps children learn the importance of attentive listening and reciprocal communication.

Regulating Conversation Through Eye Contact

Turn-Taking

- **Signal for Completion**: Eye contact often indicates when a speaker has finished

their point and invites the listener to respond. This nonverbal cue is crucial in maintaining the flow of conversation and preventing interruptions.
- **Timing and Engagement**: By observing eye contact, individuals can better time their contributions, ensuring a more natural and engaging dialogue.

Feedback Mechanism

- **Listener's Attention**: Eye contact serves as a powerful feedback mechanism, allowing speakers to gauge the listener's engagement and understanding. If a listener maintains eye contact, it typically indicates interest and attentiveness.
- **Emotional Responses**: The eyes can reflect a listener's emotional reactions, such as surprise, confusion, or agreement, providing speakers with cues to adjust their communication style or content as needed.

EYE CONTACT, DECEPTION, AND TECHNOLOGY

The dynamics of eye contact in relation to deception and technology are intricate, shaping how individuals perceive honesty and engage in communication in modern contexts:

Eye Contact and Deception

Common Misconceptions

Many people believe that avoiding eye contact is a strong indicator of lying. This perception is widespread, leading to assumptions about a person's honesty based on their eye contact behavior. Such beliefs can lead to false conclusions, as they are based on stereotypes rather than empirical evidence (Levine, 2014; Vrij, 2008).

Reality of Liars' Eye Contact

Research indicates that individuals who are lying may maintain more eye contact than usual in an attempt to appear truthful. They often believe that looking directly at someone can enhance their credibility and distract from their deceptive behavior. Some liars may consciously overcompensate by making prolonged eye contact to counteract the nervousness that often accompanies lying, which can lead to a misleading impression of honesty (Bond & DePaulo, 2006; Vrij, 2008).

Cultural Factors

Different cultures interpret eye contact in various ways. For instance, in some cultures, direct eye contact is seen as a sign of respect and confidence, while in others, it may be considered rude or confrontational. The cultural context significantly influences how eye contact is perceived in situations involving deception. Individuals from collectivist cultures might avoid direct eye contact to show respect, complicating interpretations in high-stakes situations (Levine, 2014; Vrij, 2008).

Impact of Technology on Eye Contact (Bissinger *et al.*, 2023; Duchowski, 2007)

Video Calls

The rise of video conferencing platforms has underscored the importance of eye contact in remote communication. Participants often strive to maintain eye contact with the camera to create a sense of connection with others. Despite its importance, achieving effective eye contact during video calls can be challenging. Misalignment between the camera and the screen can create the illusion of a lack of engagement, even when participants are attentive.

Social Media

Social media has transformed how people communicate, often at the expense of in-person interactions. This shift can lead to a decrease in opportunities for practicing and interpreting eye contact, potentially impacting social skills and norms. As online interactions become more prevalent, the norms surrounding eye contact may evolve. Individuals may develop new ways to express attention and interest through text, emojis, or other digital cues.

Virtual and Augmented Reality

Virtual and augmented reality platforms are introducing new challenges and opportunities for eye contact. In these environments, users may struggle with maintaining eye contact with avatars or other participants, which can affect emotional engagement and connection. Developers of virtual reality technologies are exploring ways to enhance realistic eye contact among avatars to improve social interactions, aiming to replicate the nuances of in-person communication.

STRATEGIES FOR ENHANCING ONE'S USE OF EYE CONTACT

Enhancing eye contact can improve communication, strengthen interpersonal connections, and project confidence. Research indicates that intentional and context-appropriate eye contact enhances trust and engagement in social and professional interactions. The following strategies can help refine one's use of eye contact (Argyle & Dean, 1965; Hietanen, 2018; Kleinke, 1986; Knapp, Hall, & Horgan, 2014):

Practice Active Listening

Maintain eye contact while actively listening to convey attentiveness. Subtle affirmations such as nodding or facial expressions can reinforce engagement and responsiveness in conversations.

Adjust Eye Contact Based on Context

Eye contact norms vary across social and cultural contexts. In professional settings, a steady yet natural gaze can establish credibility, while in informal interactions, adapting eye contact levels based on comfort and mutual responsiveness is essential

Use Eye Contact Exercises

Practicing with a mirror or engaging in controlled exercises with peers can help individuals build confidence in sustaining eye contact. Gradually increasing exposure through structured social interactions allows for a more natural adjustment.

Apply the 50/70 Rule

Research suggests that maintaining eye contact for about 50% of the time while speaking and 70% while listening fosters engagement without making the interaction uncomfortable (Knapp, Hall, & Horgan, 2014).

Combine Eye Contact with Open Body Language

Nonverbal cues such as uncrossed arms, relaxed posture, and facial expressiveness complement eye contact, reinforcing a welcoming and confident demeanor.

Modifying Eye Contact to Reduce Anxiety

For those uncomfortable with direct eye contact, looking near the eyes—such as the bridge of the nose or eyebrows—can create the illusion of eye contact while reducing anxiety. Shifting focus periodically between both eyes prevents fixation and enhances a balanced connection.

Use Eye Contact to Express Emotion

Prolonged eye contact can intensify emotional communication, particularly during expressions of gratitude, empathy, or sincerity. However, breaking gaze occasionally during intense discussions prevents discomfort or overwhelming the other person.

Seek Feedback and Self Monitor

Observing how others respond to one's eye contact provides insight into necessary adjustments. Feedback from colleagues or friends can help refine nonverbal communication skills.

Practice in Diverse Scenarios

Simulated interactions, such as role-playing professional interviews, networking events, or public speaking, can enhance adaptability in various settings, leading to more effective and confident communication.

CONCLUSION

Pupil dilation and eye contact are powerful forms of nonverbal communication, offering insights into emotional states, cognitive processes, and social dynamics. While pupil dilation provides a more universal, physiological response, eye contact is deeply influenced by cultural and social factors. Understanding both can significantly enhance our ability to communicate effectively and empathetically in various contexts. This detailed outline provides a comprehensive exploration of pupil dilation and eye contact.

Activity: "Pupil Detective"

In the "Pupil Detective" activity, participants analyze short video clips of close-up shots of eyes to identify emotions based on pupil movements. After observing the clips, they discuss how pupil dilation relates to emotional states and explore the potential applications and limitations of using pupillometry in real-world situations.

Duration: 40 minutes

Materials needed: Computer, projector, pre-prepared video clips focusing on eyes

Instructions:

1. Prepare 8-10 short video clips (15-20 seconds each) showing close-ups of people's eyes in various emotional states.
2. Show each clip twice.
3. After each clip, participants write down:
   - The emotion they believe the person is experiencing.
   - What pupil and eye movement cues led to their conclusion.

4. Reveal the correct emotion and discuss:
   ○ Which pupil responses correspond to different emotional states?
   ○ How might pupil dilation be useful in real-world scenarios?
   ○ What are the limitations of relying solely on pupillometry?

CHAPTER 7

Reading Emotions through Posture and Stance

Abstract: Posture and stance serve as subtle yet powerful indicators of a person's emotional and psychological state. This chapter explores the science behind how posture reflects attitudes, emotions, and intentions. Readers will learn about key posture categories, such as dominant *versus* submissive stances, and the impact of posture on self-perception and interpersonal dynamics. Research on how posture affects mood and confidence, known as the "power pose" phenomenon, is discussed, along with its implications for personal and professional communication. The chapter emphasizes cultural influences on the interpretation of posture, examining how different societies view personal space, formality, and social hierarchy. Practical applications include recognizing signs of discomfort, confidence, or openness in others and using posture to influence one's own psychological state. Real-life examples and observational exercises help readers apply these concepts in social and professional contexts. By mastering the art of reading and using posture effectively, individuals can enhance their ability to communicate nonverbally and navigate social interactions more successfully.

Keywords: Body language, Cultural influences, Emotion, Posture, Power pose, Stance.

INTRODUCTION

UNDERSTANDING THE BIOLOGICAL UNDERPINNINGS OF POSTURE

Posture and stance, often overlooked aspects of nonverbal communication, can provide rich insights into an individual's emotional state, attitudes, and intentions. This chapter explores how the way we hold and position our bodies can reveal our inner emotional landscape. Our skeleton provides the framework for our posture. The alignment of our spine, the positioning of our shoulders, and the tilt of our pelvis all contribute to our overall stance. Individual variations in skeletal structure can influence natural posture, but emotional states can cause significant deviations from this baseline (Dael *et al.*, 2012; Goman, 2011):

Yuvika Singh

- Skeletal structure and its influence on stance.
- Muscular tension and relaxation in emotional expression.
- The role of the nervous system in postural control.

Examining Common Postures and their Potential Emotional Meanings

Emotions have a direct impact on our muscular system. When we experience stress or anxiety, certain muscle groups tend to tense up, affecting our posture. Conversely, feelings of relaxation or contentment can lead to a loosening of muscular tension, resulting in a more open and fluid posture (Dael *et al.*, 2012):

Upright Posture: An erect spine, squared shoulders, and lifted chin typically convey a sense of confidence and self-assurance. This posture is often adopted when feeling proud or wanting to project authority (For example, emotions like confidence, alertness, pride, *etc.*).

Slouching: A slumped posture with rounded shoulders and a downward gaze is frequently associated with feelings of depression, exhaustion, or disengagement. This posture can both reflect and reinforce negative emotional states (For example, emotions like depression, fatigue, and lack of motivation).

Leaning Forward: Leaning towards someone or something often indicates interest or engagement. However, in certain contexts, it can also signal aggression or a desire to dominate, especially when combined with other assertive body language cues (For example, emotions like interest, engagement, and aggression).

Leaning Backward: Leaning away from a person or situation can indicate relaxation in casual settings. However, it may also suggest avoidance or skepticism, particularly in more formal or confrontational scenarios (For example, emotions like relaxation, avoidance, and skepticism).

SITTING POSITIONS AND ASSOCIATED TRAITS: CONNECTING POSTURES WITH PROFESSIONAL ATTRIBUTES

Sitting positions, often overlooked in daily interactions, serve as subtle yet powerful indicators of personality traits and emotional states. These postures, shaped by cultural norms and individual habits, communicate volumes about a person's confidence, mindset, and social attitudes. By decoding these nonverbal cues, professionals across various fields can gain deeper insights into human behavior, enabling more effective communication and decision-making. Understanding these connections is particularly valuable in professions like psychology, law enforcement, business, and leadership, where interpreting subtle signals can shape impactful outcomes. Fig. (**1**) shows a detailed analysis of common sitting postures and their implications in professional settings.

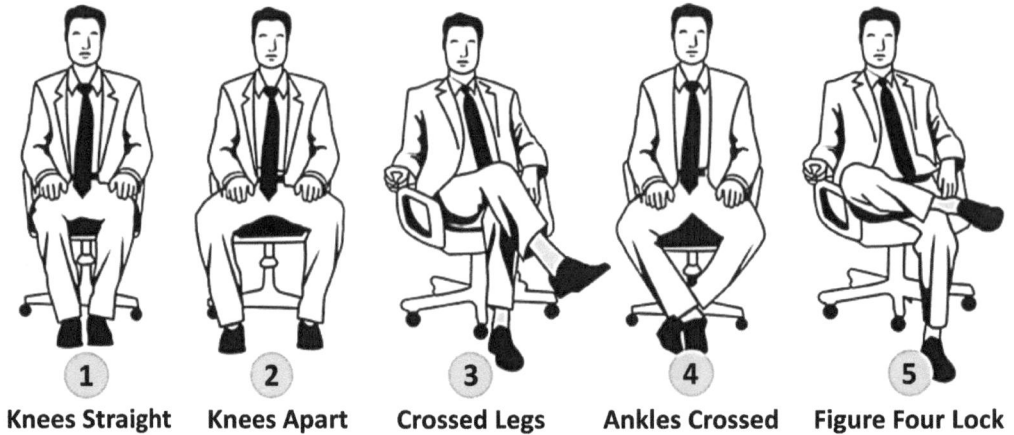

1	2	3	4	5
Knees Straight	**Knees Apart**	**Crossed Legs**	**Ankles Crossed**	**Figure Four Lock**

Fig. (1). Sitting positions and personality traits. Source: Adapted from Argyle (1988); Burgoon *et al.* (2016); Ekman (2003); Hall *et al.* (2005); Knapp *et al.*, 2013; Mehrabian (1972); Pease & Pease, 2004.

Knees Straight

Research indicates that individuals who sit with their knees straight often project an image of confidence and competence, particularly in professional settings (Knapp *et al.*, 2013). This posture is associated with a strong sense of self-efficacy and an ability to maintain composure under pressure. Studies on nonverbal communication suggest that upright, open postures correlate with perceptions of reliability and leadership qualities (Mehrabian, 1972). Such individuals tend to exhibit structured thinking, punctuality, and a commitment to maintaining order in their professional and personal lives.

Knees Apart

Sitting with knees apart may be perceived as a dominant or assertive stance, though research suggests it can also indicate underlying anxiety or perfectionistic tendencies. Individuals who adopt this posture often display high levels of cognitive engagement but may struggle with scattered attention and inconsistent focus. In the psychological literature, this posture has been linked to heightened self-awareness and a need for control over one's environment (Burgoon *et al.*, 2016). However, in certain social contexts, particularly among men, this position—commonly known as "manspreading"—can be interpreted as an attempt to assert territorial dominance (Hall *et al.*, 2005).

Crossed Legs

People who sit with their legs crossed often exhibit introspective and creative tendencies. This posture is commonly associated with individuals who are deep thinkers and prefer to process information internally before expressing their views (Pease & Pease, 2004). Research indicates that individuals who habitually sit with their legs crossed may be more reserved in social interactions, as the posture creates a subtle barrier between them and their surroundings (Argyle, 1988). Additionally, body language experts note that the direction of the crossed leg can reveal a person's engagement level—pointing towards an individual suggests attentiveness, whereas pointing away may signal disinterest (Knapp *et al.*, 2013).

Ankle Crossed

Sitting with the ankles crossed conveys an image of composure, self-restraint, and confidence. This posture is frequently associated with individuals who maintain a poised and collected demeanor in both professional and personal settings (Burgoon *et al.*, 2016). It is often observed in high-stakes situations where individuals seek to project authority and control over their emotions. However, in forensic psychology, this position has been linked to subtle signs of defensiveness or an effort to suppress discomfort (Ekman, 2003). Despite this, individuals who sit in this manner are generally regarded as diplomatic and strategic in their interactions.

Figure-Four Leg Lock

The figure-four sitting position—where one ankle rests on the opposite knees, is a strong indicator of confidence, assertiveness, and dominance. Research suggests that individuals who prefer this posture are often competitive, career-driven, and independent thinkers. This position is frequently observed in leadership roles, where individuals aim to assert their authority within group dynamics. However, it may also signal resistance to alternative viewpoints, as those who sit this way tend to be firm in their beliefs and less open to external influence (Pease & Pease, 2004). In professional environments, adopting this posture can project control and readiness but should be balanced with open body language to ensure approachability.

By analyzing sitting postures within professional settings, individuals can gain valuable insights into nonverbal communication. These findings emphasize the importance of contextual interpretation, as body language should always be assessed alongside verbal cues and situational factors. Understanding how posture influences perception can help professionals navigate social interactions more effectively, fostering stronger connections and better communication outcomes.

THE ROLE OF THE NERVOUS SYSTEM IN POSTURAL CONTROL

Our nervous system plays a crucial role in maintaining and adjusting our posture. The autonomic nervous system, which regulates involuntary bodily functions, can trigger postural changes in response to emotional stimuli. For example, the fight-or-flight response associated with fear or anger can cause an instantaneous shift in posture, preparing the body for action. While individual differences and context always play a role, certain postures are often associated with specific emotional states (Critchley, 2005; Porges, 2007):

The Power of Postural Congruence

Postural congruence refers to the alignment between one's emotional state and physical posture. When our posture matches our internal feelings, we appear more authentic, and our communication becomes more effective. Conversely, incongruence between posture and expressed emotion can lead to mixed messages and reduced trust.

- *Examples of postural congruence:*
    - Expressing excitement with an upright, energetic stance.
    - Showing sympathy by leaning in and adopting a softer posture.
- *Examples of postural incongruence:*
    - Claiming to be confident while slouching and avoiding eye contact.
    - Expressing interest verbally while leaning away from the speaker.

Sudden Postural Changes and their Meaning

Abrupt changes in posture often indicate a strong emotional response. For example, suddenly sitting up straight might signal increased interest or alertness, while quickly crossing arms could suggest defensiveness or discomfort.

Gradual Shifts in Stance and their Emotional Implications

Slow, progressive changes in posture can reveal evolving emotional states. A person gradually slouching over the course of a conversation might be losing interest or becoming fatigued.

Rhythmic Movements and their Connection to Emotional States

Repetitive movements, such as rocking or swaying, can be indicators of emotional states. Gentle rocking might suggest self-soothing behavior, while rapid, agitated movements could signal anxiety or impatience.

MIRROR NEURONS AND THEIR ROLE IN POSTURAL ECHOING

Humans have a natural tendency to unconsciously mimic the postures of those around them, a phenomenon known as s or mirroring. Research on mirror neurons suggests that these specialized brain cells fire both when an individual performs an action and when they observe someone else performing that action. This neurological mechanism is believed to be fundamental to postural echoing and social bonding (Rizzolatti & Craighero, 2004; Gallese *et al.*, 2004).

How does Postural Echoing Facilitate Emotional Understanding?

By unconsciously adopting similar postures, we can gain insight into the emotional experiences of others. This physical mimicry contributes to emotional contagion, where individuals begin to feel what others are feeling, reinforcing social connections (Hatfield *et al.*, 1994). Deliberately (but subtly) mirroring the posture of others can help establish rapport and create a sense of connection. This technique is often used in counseling, sales, and negotiation settings.

Western *vs.* Eastern Postural Norms

Western cultures often emphasize direct eye contact and upright posture as signs of confidence and engagement, while some Eastern cultures may view these behaviors as confrontational or disrespectful. In cultures with strict social hierarchies, posture can be a key indicator of social status. Subordinates may adopt more closed or lower postures in the presence of superiors. Cross-cultural studies have highlighted variations in postural expressiveness, demonstrating how different cultures use body language to signify respect, power, or intimacy (Remland *et al.*, 1991). Many cultures have different postural expectations for men and women. For example, in some societies, women may be expected to adopt more closed or modest postures compared to men.

POSTURAL ANALYSIS IN CLINICAL SETTINGS

Clinicians often observe postural cues as part of their assessment. For instance, research suggests that individuals with depression commonly exhibit slumped posture, limited gesturing, and downward gaze, while those with anxiety display rigid posture and fidgeting. Slump posture, limited gestures, and a downward gaze can be indicators of depression, while rigid posture and fidgeting might suggest anxiety. Individuals suffering from chronic pain often adopt protective postures that can impact their emotional expression and how others perceive them emotionally. Some therapeutic approaches incorporate postural exercises to help alleviate symptoms of depression and anxiety based on the bidirectional relationship between posture and emotion. The embodied cognition perspective suggests that altering posture can influence emotional states, supporting the use of postural interventions in psychological treatments (Michalak *et al*., 2014).

POSTURE AND OTHER NONVERBAL CUES

Congruence and incongruence in nonverbal signals: When posture aligns with facial expressions, gestures, and tone of voice, the overall message is stronger and more credible. Incongruence between these elements can create confusion or suggest deception.

The dominance of postural cues in mixed messages: In situations where different nonverbal cues contradict each other, postural signals often take precedence in how the message is interpreted, possibly due to their larger visual impact and the difficulty in consciously controlling posture (Burgoon *et al*., 2016).

Using posture to enhance or moderate other nonverbal signals: Skilled communicators can use posture to amplify or soften other nonverbal cues. For example, leaning in can intensify the impact of a smile, while a relaxed posture can moderate an otherwise stern facial expression.

Posture in Social Dominance and Submission

Posture plays a crucial role in communicating social status and power dynamics. Expansive postures, where individuals take up more space, are often associated with dominance and high status. Contractive postures, where people make themselves smaller, can signal submission or lower status. Studies have shown that adopting expansive postures can increase feelings of confidence and power, while contractive postures can induce submissive behaviors (Carney *et al*., 2010).

- Dominant postures might include standing tall with hands on hips or leaning over a desk.
- Submissive postures could involve hunched shoulders or averting the gaze.
- In group settings, individuals often unconsciously adjust their postures to reflect the perceived social hierarchy, with those of higher status adopting more dominant postures.

Modern technology is changing our posture and, consequently, how we express and perceive emotions. The "text neck" phenomenon, where prolonged smartphone use leads to a hunched posture, has been linked to increased stress and reduced assertiveness in social settings. In video calls, posture becomes even more critical as other nonverbal cues are limited. Sitting up straight and leaning slightly towards the camera can help convey engagement and confidence. Wearable devices and biofeedback systems are increasingly being used to monitor posture and correct misalignments, influencing both physical well-being and social perception (Hansraj, 2014).

CONCLUSION

Posture and stance offer a wealth of information about our emotional states, often communicating what words cannot. By developing a deeper understanding of postural communication, we can enhance our emotional intelligence and improve our interpersonal relationships. Whether in personal interactions, professional settings, or therapeutic contexts, the ability to read and consciously modulate our posture provides a powerful tool for more effective and empathetic communication.

Class Activity: "Posture Personas"

In the "Posture Personas" activity, participants adopt physical postures that reflect different emotions, which others then try to identify. After each round, the group discusses the posture cues linked to emotions, how these may vary culturally, and the value of recognizing such cues in professional contexts.

Duration: 45 minutes

Materials needed: Cards with emotional words, open space for movement.

Instructions:

1. Create cards with various emotions (*e.g.*, confidence, shame, excitement, exhaustion).
2. Participants draw a card and adopt a posture that reflects the emotion without revealing their card.
3. Others observe and try to identify the emotion.
4. After each round, discuss:
   - What specific posture cues indicate the emotion?
   - How might this emotion be expressed differently across cultures?
   - In what professional situations might recognizing these postures be valuable?

CHAPTER 8

Detecting Deception through Nonverbal Signals

Abstract: Detecting deception is a crucial skill in many areas of life, from law enforcement to everyday interactions. This chapter delves into the nonverbal signals commonly associated with lying, such as micro-expressions, inconsistent body language, and changes in vocal tone. It explores psychological theories explaining why people exhibit telltale signs of deception and the factors that influence these behaviors. The role of stress, cognitive load, and emotional leakage in telling a lie is analyzed, providing readers with a deeper understanding of the challenges involved in accurate lie detection. The chapter discusses scientific studies that identify reliable and unreliable cues and introduces practical techniques used by professionals, such as the Behavioral Analysis Interview and Statement Analysis. Emphasis is placed on the importance of considering the context and avoiding overreliance on any single cue. Real-world scenarios, including police interrogations and high-stakes negotiations, illustrate how deception detection works in practice. Readers will also learn ethical considerations and the limitations of nonverbal lie detection.

Keywords: Cognitive load, Deception detection, Lie detection, Micro-expressions, Nonverbal cues.

INTRODUCTION

Deception detection is a complex field that has fascinated researchers, law enforcement professionals, and the public for decades. While previous chapters have explored various aspects of nonverbal communication, this chapter focuses specifically on how these signals can be used to detect deception. It is important to note that no single nonverbal cue is a definitive indicator of lying; rather, it is the combination and context of multiple signals that can suggest deceptive behavior.

THE COGNITIVE APPROACH TO DECEPTION DETECTION

The cognitive approach to deception detection emphasizes the mental processes involved in lying rather than solely relying on emotional cues. Here are some key concepts and findings related to this approach (Honts *et al*., 2009; Levine, T. R. (2014).

Yuvika Singh

Cognitive Load Theory

Lying often requires greater cognitive resources compared to telling the truth because it involves fabricating information, maintaining the lie, and managing the risk of being caught (Vrij, 2008; Levine, 2014). This increased mental effort can lead to observable nonverbal and verbal cues, which can be indicators of deception (Bond & DePaulo, 2006). Cognitive Load Theory (CLT) addresses the mental effort required to process information during learning. The research suggests that human memory, especially our working memory, has a limited capacity. This means that instructional methods should be designed to avoid overloading working memory, allowing learners to focus on relevant information that promotes meaningful learning outcomes. CLT is particularly concerned with optimizing instructional design to support effective information processing and retention (Sweller *et al.*, 2011).

Cognitive load refers to the amount of mental effort required to process information. This load, or burden, is managed by working memory—a system with a limited capacity that holds information temporarily for immediate use. During learning, working memory helps students hold and manipulate bits of information, such as those presented in a classroom, to understand and retain content. Because of working memory limitations, instructional designs that demand excessive mental effort can hinder learning (Sweller *et al.*, 2011; Vrij, 2008). For example, complex instructions or excessive information can quickly overwhelm learners, reducing the likelihood that they will retain the material. Efficient instructional design must consider cognitive load to enhance learning and prevent overload (Levine, 2014) (Fig. **1**).

Types of Cognitive Load

1. **Intrinsic Load**: This is the inherent difficulty of the material itself, determined by the complexity of the content and the learner's prior knowledge (Sweller *et al.*, 2011).
2. **Extraneous Load**: This refers to the mental effort required due to the way information is presented. Poorly organized information, distracting visuals, or complex instructions increase the extraneous load, which should be minimized to optimize learning (Honts *et al.*, 2009).

3. **Germane Load**: This type of load represents the mental effort invested in processing and understanding information, thereby supporting learning.

   Effective instructional design aims to maximize germane load while minimizing extraneous load (Vrij, 2008).

Intrinsic cognitive load
(simplifies the complex new information)

Germane cognitive load
(deep processing of new information by integrating it with previous learning)

Extraneous cognitive load
(distracts working memory from processing new information by reducing the information)

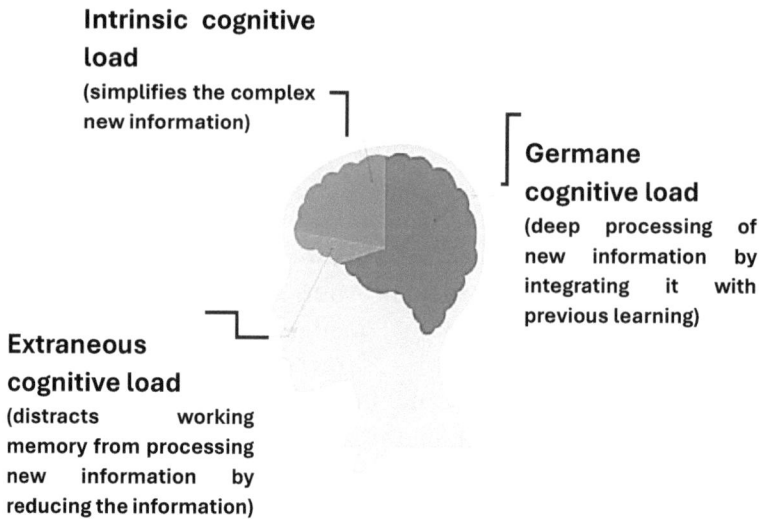

Fig. (1). Cognitive load. Source: Adapted by Bond & DePaulo (2006); Honts *et al.* (2009); Levine (2014); Sweller *et al.* (2011); Vrij (2008).

Working Memory and Deception

When individuals lie, they must keep track of multiple details, including the fabricated information and the true story they must conceal. This can overload their working memory (Higbee, 2001). As working memory becomes strained, liars may display specific behaviors, such as:

- **Decreased Blink Rate**: Liars often blink less frequently, possibly due to increased focus on controlling their expressions and avoiding detection (Ekman, 2009).
- **Simplified Language**: To manage cognitive load, liars may use less complex language and reduce the use of descriptive details (DePaulo *et al.*, 2003).
- **Reduced Animation**: A liar's overall expressiveness may decrease; they might appear less animated or engaged in the conversation (Vrij, 2008).
- **Increased Speech Errors**: Cognitive strain may lead to more hesitations, pauses, and errors in speech as individuals struggle to maintain their deception (Levine, 2014).

A study also demonstrated that when participants were asked to recount their stories in reverse chronological order, the increased cognitive load made it easier to detect deception. This method forces the liar to reconstruct their narrative while managing the complexities of their lie, leading to more detectable cues (Vrij *et al.*, 2008).

Key Indicators of Deception

Based on cognitive load theory and research findings, several indicators can signal potential deception (Bond & DePaulo, 2006; Levine, 2014):

Behavioral Cues

- **Decreased Blink Rate**: Less frequent blinking may suggest stress or cognitive overload.
- **Simplified Gestures**: Fewer hand gestures and more rigid body language can indicate discomfort or cognitive strain.
- **Lower Vocal Variety**: Monotone speech or reduced changes in pitch may reflect an effort to control emotions.

Verbal Cues

- **Increased Pauses**: Longer pauses before responding can signal that the individual is processing information or constructing a lie.
- **Less Detail**: Providing vague responses or avoiding specific details can indicate an attempt to conceal the truth.

STRATEGIC SELF-PRESENTATION IN DECEPTION

Liars often attempt to manage their nonverbal behavior. When individuals engage in deception, they often consciously or unconsciously manage their nonverbal behavior to appear more credible (DePaulo *et al.*, 2003; Vrij, 2008). This strategic self-presentation can lead to several distinctive patterns in their demeanor and communication style.

Overcompensation

Liars may overcorrect their nonverbal signals in an attempt to convey honesty and trustworthiness. To counter the stereotype that liars avoid eye contact, they might maintain prolonged eye contact, which can come off as forced or unnatural (Zuckerman & Driver, 1985). They may use more hand movements or facial expressions than usual, trying to appear more engaged and sincere. This effort can result in behavior that feels insincere or inconsistent, drawing suspicion rather than fostering trust (Vrij, 2008).

Controlled Behavior

Liars may deliberately minimize their nonverbal expressions to avoid drawing attention to potential cues of deception (Ekman, 2009). They may limit natural movements and expressions to maintain control over their presentation, leading to a robotic or stiff demeanor (Levine, 2014). A decrease in gestures can indicate an effort to suppress any signals that could reveal their deceit. While the intention is to appear composed, this control can paradoxically signal nervousness or discomfort to observant listeners (Vrij, 2008).

Rehearsed Responses

Liars often prepare and rehearse their narratives to ensure consistency and reduce the likelihood of being caught in a lie (DePaulo *et al.*, 2003). When recounting their story multiple times, they may provide similar phrasing and structure, leading to a sense of monotony in their delivery. Their responses may follow a scripted feel, lacking the nuances and spontaneity found in genuine conversation (Bond & DePaulo, 2006). This predictability can raise red flags, as people tend to pick up on the absence of authenticity in their storytelling.

ADVANCED TECHNIQUES IN NONVERBAL DECEPTION DETECTION

Advanced techniques in nonverbal deception detection focus on uncovering hidden truths through subtle behavioral cues. These approaches build on psychological and physiological insights, identifying micro-expressions, gaze shifts, and body language irregularities that reveal underlying emotions or dishonesty (Honts *et al.*, 2009). By analyzing these signals, professionals can improve their ability to detect deception in critical contexts through the following methods:

Automated Facial Expression Analysis

Automated facial expression analysis (AFEA) involves using sophisticated software to analyze facial movements and expressions to detect emotions. The technology leverages artificial intelligence (AI) and machine learning algorithms to identify micro-expressions—brief, involuntary facial expressions that reveal true emotions. These systems typically use cameras to capture facial data and then analyze it in real-time or post-event (Honts, 2009).

Key Components Include:

- *Facial Landmark Detection*: Identifying key points on the face, such as eyes, nose, and mouth.

- *Emotion Recognition:* Classifying expressions into basic emotions like happiness, sadness, anger, surprise, fear, and disgust.

• *Micro-Expression Detection:* Spotting fleeting expressions that may indicate underlying emotions not openly expressed.

APPLICATIONS IN VIRTUAL MEETINGS AND INTERVIEWS

Affective Facial Expression Analysis (AFEA) leverages nonverbal cues to assess emotional responses and enhance communication effectiveness (Bissinger *et al.*, 2023). In management contexts, especially during virtual interactions, AFEA can play a crucial role in various scenarios:

Remote Hiring

During virtual interviews, AFEA enables recruiters to observe candidates' facial expressions and emotional responses in real time (Honts *et al.*, 2009). Candidates may attempt to conceal nervousness or uncertainty. AFEA can highlight subtle expressions that reveal genuine feelings about their qualifications or the position. By analyzing emotional reactions to questions, recruiters can gain insights into candidates' confidence, enthusiasm, or discomfort, facilitating more informed hiring decisions (Vrij, 2008).

Performance Reviews

Managers can utilize AFEA during virtual performance reviews to interpret employees' nonverbal feedback. Understanding an employee's emotional response to feedback—whether positive or negative—can help managers adjust their approach, making it more supportive and effective (Bissinger *et al.*, 2023). AFEA can encourage a more engaging conversation, as managers can address any visible discomfort, allowing for clarification and a more constructive discussion.

Negotiations

In virtual business negotiations, AFEA can be instrumental in detecting nonverbal signs of discomfort, reluctance, or deceit (Levine, 2014). If AFEA indicates that a counterpart is displaying signs of stress or uncertainty, managers can modify their negotiation strategy accordingly, potentially easing tensions or clarifying misunderstandings. By demonstrating awareness of emotional cues, negotiators can build rapport and trust, enhancing the overall effectiveness of the negotiation process.

How does Thermal Imaging Work?

Thermal imaging technology detects infrared radiation (heat) emitted by objects. In humans, stress and deception can cause subtle changes in facial temperature (Honts *et al.*, 2009; Ioannou *et al.*, 2014). Thermal cameras capture these temperature variations, which are then analyzed to identify stress-related changes.

Infrared Sensors

Thermal cameras are equipped with infrared sensors that can detect infrared radiation emitted by all objects based on their temperature. These sensors convert thermal radiation into electrical signals, which are then processed to create thermal images that represent temperature distribution across the observed scene (Ioannou *et al.*, 2014).

Temperature Analysis

The thermal imaging system analyzes temperature variations to identify patterns associated with stress or deception. Specific areas, such as around the eyes or forehead, may show increased temperatures due to physiological changes associated with stress or emotional arousal. For example, increased blood flow or sweat production can lead to elevated temperatures in these areas, signaling stress or anxiety (Honts *et al.*, 2009).

Real-time Monitoring

One of the key advantages of thermal imaging is its ability to provide continuous, real-time monitoring of an individual's thermal profile. This allows for instant feedback on physiological responses, which can be particularly useful in dynamic situations such as negotiations (Vrij, 2008).

APPLICATIONS IN HIGH-STAKES BUSINESS NEGOTIATIONS

By capturing thermal images, negotiators can ***detect stress-induced temperature changes*** in their opponents or themselves. Sudden increases in temperature around key areas (*e.g.*, the face) may indicate pressure or discomfort, which can provide valuable insights into the emotional state of the other party (Benson & Kirby, 2019).

Understanding when opponents exhibit signs of stress or deception can help negotiators make ***more informed decisions***. For example, if a negotiator shows signs of discomfort when discussing certain topics, it may indicate areas of concern or potential bluffing (Levine, 2014).

In mediation scenarios, thermal imaging can ***reveal the true emotional states*** of the involved parties, facilitating more effective conflict resolution. By understanding the underlying stress or anxiety levels, mediators can tailor their approach to address emotional needs, potentially leading to a more constructive dialogue (Lazarus, 1991).

Understanding Vocal Stress Patterns

Voice stress analysis (VSA) focuses on detecting changes in a person's voice that may indicate stress or deception. These changes are often involuntary and can include variations in pitch, tone, and speech rate. The underlying principle is that psychological stress affects the vocal cords, leading to detectable alterations in the voice (Goberman & Coelho, 2002; Scherer, 2003).

Key Elements Include

- *Microtremors:* Tiny, involuntary tremors in the voice that increase under stress.
- *Pitch and Tone Variations:* Stress can cause higher pitch and changes in tone.
- *Speech Rate:* Deceptive individuals might speak more quickly or slowly than usual.

Tools and Methods for Real-Time Analysis in Management Settings In management settings, VSA can be employed through various tools and methods for real-time analysis (DePaulo *et al.*, 2003; Honts *et al.*, 2009; Vrij, 2008):

- *Software Solutions:* There are several VSA software applications available that can analyze voice patterns during conversations, interviews, or meetings.
- *Integrated Systems:* Combining VSA with other biometric tools (like facial recognition and thermal imaging) provides a comprehensive approach to the detection of deception.
- *Practical Applications:*
  - *Interviews and Screenings:* During job interviews or internal investigations, VSA can help identify candidates or employees who might be hiding information or lying.
  - *Customer Interactions:* In customer service settings, VSA can detect stress or dissatisfaction in callers, allowing representatives to respond more effectively.
  - *Team Meetings*: Managers can use VSA to gauge the authenticity of feedback and responses during team meetings, ensuring honest communication.

CONCLUSION

Detecting deception through nonverbal signals remains a challenging and complex field. While no infallible method exists, understanding the cognitive processes behind lying, recognizing potential behavioral indicators, and considering contextual factors can enhance our ability to discern truth from deception. As technology advances and our understanding of human behavior deepens, the field of nonverbal deception detection continues to evolve, offering both promising possibilities and ethical challenges.

Class Activity: "Truth or Lie?"

In the "Truth or Lie?" activity, participants write two truths and one lie about themselves, then share their statements in small groups while others observe their nonverbal cues. The goal is for group members to identify the lie based on nonverbal signals, such as facial expressions and body language, and discuss how these cues can be applied ethically in professional settings.

Duration: 50 minutes

Materials needed: Notepads, pens

Instructions:

1. Participants write down three statements about themselves: two truths and one lie.
2. In small groups, each person reads their statements while others observe nonverbal cues (such as eye movements, facial expressions, body posture, and gestures).
3. Group members try to identify the lie, explaining their reasoning based on nonverbal signals.
4. After everyone has shared, discuss as a larger group:
   ◦ What nonverbal cues were most indicative of deception?
   ◦ Were there any surprising results or misconceptions about lying?
   ◦ How can this knowledge be applied ethically in professional settings?

CHAPTER 9

Sharpening Your Observation Skills

Abstract: Observation is a critical skill for interpreting nonverbal communication effectively. This chapter offers a step-by-step guide to honing observational abilities, emphasizing the importance of awareness, mindfulness, and attention to detail. Techniques such as the memory palace technique are introduced to help readers systematically assess situations and respond appropriately. Readers will explore exercises that train them to notice subtle cues in body language, facial expressions, and environmental context, enhancing their ability to read people and situations accurately. The chapter highlights common cognitive biases, like confirmation bias and the halo effect, that can cloud judgment and offers strategies to overcome these pitfalls. Emphasis is placed on situational awareness and the skill of reading nonverbal cues in context rather than isolation. Examples from law enforcement, clinical psychology, and business negotiations illustrate the practical benefits of enhanced observation. By developing a sharper eye for detail, readers can improve their interpersonal effectiveness and make more informed decisions in social and professional settings.

Keywords: Cognitive biases, Five senses approach, Observation skills, Situational awareness.

INTRODUCTION

In our fast-paced world, the ability to keenly observe nonverbal communication is often overlooked, yet it remains one of the most powerful tools at our disposal. Observation of subtle cues and gestures is the gateway to understanding human behavior, emotional intelligence, and interpersonal effectiveness. It is the foundation upon which successful communicators build rapport, negotiators reach agreements, and therapists understand their clients. While observation skills benefit everyone, mastering the art of reading nonverbal cues can transform the way we interact with others and understand human behavior (Allen, 2021).

UNDERSTANDING THE IMPORTANCE OF NONVERBAL OBSERVATION

Observation in human communication goes far beyond just seeing—it is a multi-sensory, active process of gathering information about others' behaviors,

Yuvika Singh

emotions, and intentions. The benefits of strong nonverbal observation skills include (Allen, 2021):

Enhanced Interpersonal Understanding

Strong observation skills enable individuals to identify subtle patterns in behavior and microexpressions that can reveal true emotions and intentions. For instance, a counselor noting a client's slight shoulder tension might detect underlying anxiety that hasn't been verbally expressed.

Professional Effectiveness

In professional settings, the ability to read nonverbal cues can lead to more successful negotiations, better team management, and more effective client relationships. A sales professional who notices a potential client's unconscious nodding patterns can better their closing strategies.

Greater Emotional Intelligence

By developing keen observation skills, individuals can better recognize and respond to others' emotional states, leading to more empathetic and effective interactions.

However, several barriers often prevent effective observation, which will be discussed further.

BARRIERS TO EFFECTIVE OBSERVATION

Observation skills are vital for effective decision-making, yet they are often hindered by psychological and environmental barriers. Inattentional blindness, confirmation bias, habituation, and distractions are common challenges that can impair perception and awareness. Understanding these barriers and implementing strategies to counteract them, such as mindfulness and seeking diverse perspectives, can significantly enhance observational capabilities (Benson & Kirby, 2019; Cheung *et al.*, 2019):

Inattentional Blindness

This phenomenon occurs when individuals fail to notice unexpected stimuli in their environment because their focus is directed elsewhere. It highlights the limits of human attention and perception. A classic example is the "invisible gorilla" experiment, where participants watching a basketball game failed to see a person in a gorilla suit walking across the screen because they were focused on counting the passes. To combat inattentional blindness, practice shifting your attention regularly and engaging in activities that require full awareness of your surroundings, such as mindfulness exercises or situational awareness drills (Ambady & Weisbuch, 2010).

Confirmation Bias

These cognitive biases lead individuals to favor information that aligns with their existing beliefs or hypotheses, causing them to overlook or dismiss evidence that contradicts their views. A manager who believes a particular team member is underperforming may only notice their mistakes while ignoring their contributions, thereby reinforcing a negative perception. Challenge yourself to seek out diverse perspectives and actively look for evidence that contradicts your beliefs. Encourage open discussions where differing opinions are valued and considered (Cheung *et al.*, 2019; Hall *et al.*, 2005).

Habituation

Habituation occurs when individuals become desensitized to stimuli in their environment due to repeated exposure, leading to a lack of awareness of details that were once noticeable. A person living near a train track may become so accustomed to the sound of trains that they no longer notice the noise, which can impact their ability to hear other important sounds. Regularly change your environment or routine to renew your awareness of your surroundings (Langer, 1989). Engaging in activities like walking in different locations or practicing daily reflection can help refresh your observational skills.

Distractions

The constant presence of digital devices, multitasking, and other interruptions can divert attention away from the task at hand, reducing the ability to observe details effectively. In a meeting, someone might be checking their phone or responding to emails, causing them to miss important points discussed by colleagues (Cheung *et al.*, 2019). Set specific times to check devices and practice focused attention by minimizing multitasking. Use techniques like the Pomodoro Technique to structure work periods with breaks, allowing for sustained focus on observations (Bailey & Konstan, 2006).

Recognizing these barriers is the first step in overcoming them and developing stronger observation skills.

THE FIVE SENSES APPROACH

To truly master observation, we must engage in all our senses. While sight often dominates our perception, incorporating our other senses can provide a richer, more complete understanding of our environment (Proske & Gandevia, 2012).

Sight: Sight serves as our primary means of gathering information, allowing us to interpret the world through visual cues. It enables us to observe body language, facial expressions, and environmental context, forming the basis for nonverbal communication. Visual observation helps us detect emotions, assess intentions, and understand social dynamics, often influencing our reactions and decisions. By paying attention to subtle details like eye movements, gestures, and posture, we can enhance our understanding of interactions and improve our ability to connect and communicate effectively with others (Ekman, 2003; Ambady *et al.*, 2002). To enhance visual observation, one must:

- *Practice Scanning:* Quickly sweep your eyes across a scene to get an overall impression.
- *Focus on Details:* After scanning, concentrate on specific elements, noting colors, shapes, and textures.
- *Look for Patterns and Anomalies:* Train your eye to spot recurring elements and things that stand out as different.
- *Use Peripheral Vision:* Be aware of what is happening at the edges of your visual field.
- *Exercise*: Choose a familiar room in your home. Set a timer for two minutes and try to notice as many new details as possible. Write them down and compare them with previous observations.

Sound: Sound plays a crucial role in how we perceive and understand our surroundings, offering information beyond just spoken words. Our auditory environment includes tone of voice, volume, pitch, and even the rhythm of speech, all of which contribute to interpreting emotions and intentions. Background noises and ambient sounds can also provide context or trigger specific reactions. By tuning into these auditory cues, we gain insights into others' feelings and the overall atmosphere, often subconsciously shaping our perceptions and interactions (Scherer, 2003). Our auditory environment provides a wealth of information that we often overlook.

- *Practice Active Listening:* Focus intently on sounds, trying to identify their sources and characteristics.
- *Isolated Sounds:* In a noisy environment, try to pick out individual sounds and focus on them.
- *Notice Silence:* Pay attention to the absence of sound and what it might indicate.
- *Exercise:* Spend five minutes with your eyes closed in a public place, focusing only on the sounds around you. Try to identify as many distinct sounds as possible and their potential sources.

Touch is also known as tactile observation: Through physical contact, we can perceive texture, temperature, pressure, and even emotional states, such as tension or warmth in a handshake. The sense of touch helps to build connections and convey feelings, often communicating messages that words cannot. It also plays a crucial role in how we experience and react to our environment, adding a layer of depth to our interactions and understanding (Argyle, 1988). Our sense of touch can provide unique insights into our environment:

- *Explore Textures:* Use your fingertips to feel different surfaces, noting their characteristics.
- *Be Aware of Temperature:* Pay attention to changes in temperature as you move through different environments.
- *Notice Pressure:* Be conscious of the pressure of objects against your skin and how it changes with movement.
- *Exercise:* Create a "mystery bag" filled with various small objects. Without looking, try to identify each object using only your sense of touch.

Smell is also known as an olfactory observation: It is a powerful sense that connects deeply to our memories and emotions (Hess, 1975). Certain scents can instantly evoke vivid recollections or strong feelings, often transporting us back to specific moments in time. Smell also plays a role in nonverbal communication, subtly influencing our perceptions and reactions to people and places (Gilchrist, 2011). From detecting danger, like the scent of smoke, to feeling comforted by a familiar fragrance, our sense of smell adds an emotional dimension to our experiences and environment.

- *Identify and Describe Scents:* Practice putting words to the smells you encounter.
- *Notice Changes in Smell:* Be aware of how scents change as you move through different areas.
- *Connect Smells to Memories:* Try to recall past experiences associated with scents.
- *Exercise:* Visit a place with varied scents, like a garden or market. Close your eyes and try to identify as many distinct smells as possible.

Taste is the Gustatory Observation: Taste, or gustatory observation, contributes to our overall understanding of our environment, even if it is less commonly used for everyday observations. The sense of taste can provide important cues about the safety or quality of what we consume, such as detecting spoiled or bitter foods. It can also evoke emotions and memories, like smell, enriching our sensory experiences (Higbee, 2001). Although limited in scope, honing our awareness of taste can complement and deepen our overall perceptual skills, adding another layer to our sensory observations:

- *Practice Flavor Profiling:* When eating, try to identify individual flavors and how they combine.
- *Notice Texture in Food:* Pay attention to the mouthfeel of different foods.
- *Be Aware of Aftertaste:* Notice how flavors linger and change after swallowing.
- *Exercise:* Conduct a blind taste test with different varieties of food (*e.g.*, apples or chocolates). Try to describe and differentiate between them using only your sense of taste.

Mindfulness and Presence: Mindfulness—the practice of being fully present and engaged in the current moment—is crucial for effective observation. This practice enhances observational skills by sharpening focus and allowing for greater awareness of both external surroundings and internal reactions. Mindfulness helps in noticing subtle details and nonverbal cues that might otherwise be missed, enriching our understanding and responsiveness. By cultivating mindfulness, we become more attuned to our environment and interactions, enabling us to observe more accurately and respond thoughtfully, fostering better communication and deeper connections. When we are mindful, we are more likely to notice details and nuances that we might otherwise miss. Techniques for cultivating mindfulness include (Langer, 1989):

- *Meditation:* Regular meditation practice can improve your ability to focus and be present.
- *Breathing Exercises:* Simple breathing techniques can help center your attention.
- *Body Scans:* Systematically focusing on different parts of your body can increase overall awareness.
- *Mindful Walking:* Practice being fully aware of your surroundings as you walk.

Memory and Recall: Memory and recall are fundamental to strong observation skills, as they enable us to store and later retrieve the details we observe. Effective observation involves not just noticing but also encoding information in a way that makes it easily accessible. By strengthening memory through techniques like repetition, association, or visualization, we can improve our ability to recall past observations. This enhances our overall understanding, allowing us to connect insights, recognize patterns, and make informed decisions based on previously observed data. To improve your ability to remember what you observe (Higbee, 2001):

- *Use Visualization Techniques:* Create vivid mental images of what you observe.
- *Practice Association:* Connect new observations to existing knowledge or memories.
- *Employ Mnemonic Devices:* Use acronyms, rhymes, or other memory aids to retain information.
- *Engage Multiple Senses:* The more senses involved in an observation, the more likely you are to remember it.

UNDERSTANDING "MEMORY PALACE" TECHNIQUE

The **"memory palace" technique**, also known as the **method of loci**, is a powerful mnemonic device that leverages spatial memory to enhance recall. This technique involves associating information with specific locations within an imagined or familiar space, such as a palace or a route through your home. By visualizing these locations and placing pieces of information within them, you create a mental map that makes retrieval easier. When you need to recall the information, you mentally walk through the space, retrieving each piece of data as you reach its designated spot. This method exploits the brain's natural ability to remember spatial relationships, making it particularly effective for memorizing lists, speeches, or complex concepts. Over time, the memory palace can become a versatile tool for enhancing memory and boosting overall cognitive performance (Higbee, 2001; Huttner & Robra-Bissantz, 2017). Here is a more detailed explanation of how it works, its benefits, and tips for using it effectively.

How the Memory Palace Technique Works?

Choose Your Memory Palace

Select a place you know well, like your home, school, or a regular walking route. Familiarity with space helps you visualize its details naturally so you can focus on anchoring information. A familiar setting reduces the cognitive load needed to remember the structure of the palace itself, freeing up mental energy for storing information (Higbee, 2001) (Fig. **1**).

Identify Specific Locations

Identify specific locations within your chosen space that are easy to visualize and distinct from each other. If you chose your home, for example, you might use individual rooms (like the kitchen or living room) and notable objects within them (like a refrigerator or bookshelf). By establishing clear landmarks, you create "stops" where your information will be stored, enhancing the ease of recall later (Huttner & Robra-Bissantz, 2017).

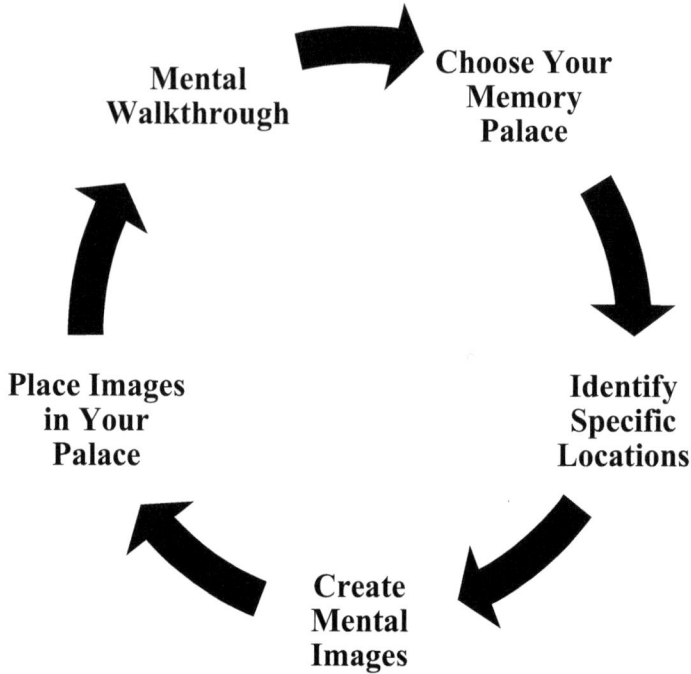

Fig. (1). Process of memory palace technique. Source: Adapted from Higbee (2001); Huttner & Robra-Bissantz (2017); Langer (1989)

Create Mental Images

For each piece of information, create a vivid, memorable image that represents it. The image should be unusual, colorful, or emotionally charged—anything that makes it stand out. For example, if you want to remember an item like "bananas," you might visualize a giant, bright yellow banana floating in the kitchen. The more exaggerated the image, the easier it is to remember (Higbee, 2001).

Place Images in Your Palace

Assign each mental image to a specific location within your memory palace. If you're memorizing a list, place each item sequentially in different locations. This spatial placement creates associations between the image and its physical "anchor" in your mind. These anchors help you mentally organize information and provide cues that make recalling each item easier (Langer, 1989).

Mental Walkthrough

To retrieve your information, mentally walk through your memory palace in the same order in which you placed the images. As you pass each location, recall the image you placed there. This "mental journey" triggers the memory of each observation through spatial and visual cues, enhancing recall accuracy and fluency (Higbee, 2001).

HOW IS THE MEMORY PALACE TECHNIQUE HELPFUL?

The Memory Palace technique is a powerful tool that enhances memory by associating information with specific locations in an imagined space, such as a familiar house or building. This technique is especially valuable in academic settings for memorizing complex information, like vocabulary or historical events, and is widely used in professions such as law, medicine, and public speaking, where organized recall is essential. It also benefits creatives and professionals by helping with tasks like storyboarding, case memorization, and personal organization. By visualizing information within a structured layout, individuals can access details more intuitively, enhancing their memory retention across diverse applications. This technique works best when users practice regularly and use vivid, memorable imagery to strengthen mental associations (Higbee, 2001; Huttner & Robra-Bissantz, 2017).

Applying the Memory Palace

Imagine you want to remember a grocery list: apples, bread, milk, and cheese. Here's how you could apply the memory palace technique:

1. **Choose Your Palace**: Your home.
2. **Identify Locations**: Front door, kitchen counter, refrigerator, dining table.
3. **Create Images**:
    ◦ Apples: A giant apple sitting at the front door.
    ◦ Bread: A loaf of bread dancing on the kitchen counter.
    ◦ Milk: A carton of milk doing a handstand in the refrigerator.
    ◦ Cheese: A cheese wheel wearing a party hat on the dining table.
4. **Place Images**: Visualize each item at its designated location.
5. **Recall**: Mentally walk through your home, encountering each item and recalling its associated observation.

Tools to Enhance Observation and Memory

While the Memory Palace Technique is primarily a mental process, various tools can enhance observational skills (Ekman, 2009; Gilchrist, 2001; Higbee, 2001; Huttner& Robra-Bissantz, 2017; Langer, 1989):

Notebooks and Journals

Create sections for different senses or types of observations (*e.g.*, nature, people, urban environments). Include prompts to guide your observations, such as focusing on sounds, smells, or interactions. Encourage reflective writing after observations to deepen insights and improve retention.

Photography and Sketching

Use cameras or smartphones to capture visual details, enabling you to analyze them later. Consider using photo-editing tools to enhance specific features or focus on details. Practice sketching objects, people, or scenes to improve visual memory and observational accuracy. It forces you to pay attention to details and nuances.

Digital Apps

Capture audio observations or thoughts on the go. This is particularly useful in situations where writing isn't feasible. Use apps like Evernote or OneNote to create multimedia observation logs, incorporating text, images, and audio. Engage with apps like iNaturalist or eBird that guide structured observations of nature, allowing you to contribute to scientific research while enhancing your observational skills.

Wearable Technology

Devices like Google Glass can record and overlay information onto your field of view, allowing for real-time documentation of observations. While primarily designed for health monitoring, some fitness trackers can also collect environmental data (like temperature or elevation), enhancing your awareness of context during observations.

Video Analysis Tools

Record interactions or events for later analysis. Review footage to identify nonverbal cues, body language, or subtle behaviors that may be missed in real time. Use tools to annotate videos, highlighting specific observations or patterns as you analyze the footage.

Virtual Reality (VR) and Augmented Reality (AR)

Use virtual reality simulations to practice observational skills in controlled environments, such as observing social interactions or wildlife in their habitats. Apps that overlay digital information onto real-world environments can enhance observational skills by providing context or additional layers of information about what you're observing.

Mind Mapping Tools

Use tools like MindMeister or XMind to organize observations visually. Create mind maps that connect different observations and insights, helping to identify patterns or relationships.

Observation Frameworks and Checklists

Create or use existing checklists tailored to specific contexts (*e.g.*, nature observation, social settings) to ensure comprehensive observation. Adopt frameworks like the PESTLE analysis (Political, Economic, Social, Technological, Legal, Environmental) to structure observations in business or environmental contexts.

Workshops and Courses

Attend workshops or online courses focused on observational skills, photography, sketching, or specific fields (like wildlife observation) to enhance your skills through guided practice.

THE CLEVER HANS PHENOMENON: A LESSON IN SUBTLE CUES

The story of Clever Hans, a horse in early 20th-century Germany, provides a fascinating illustration of the power of nonverbal observation. Hans appeared to solve complex mathematical problems by tapping his hoof to indicate numbers. However, psychologist Oskar Pfungst discovered that the horse was actually responding to subtle, unconscious cues from his handlers and audience. When people asked Hans a question, they would unconsciously lean forward slightly in anticipation of the correct answer. As Hans approached the right number of taps, they would make minute head movements or changes in facial expression. When he reached the correct number, they would straighten up slightly, signaling him to stop. Hans had learned to detect these incredibly subtle behavioral cues that even the humans themselves were unaware of making (Ekman, 2009; Pfungst, 1911). This remarkable case demonstrates several key insights about observation:

1. Nonverbal cues can be incredibly subtle yet powerful as tiny, unconscious movements can convey significant information.
2. We often communicate unconsciously through our body language as many gestures and expressions occur below the level of conscious awareness.
3. With practice, observation skills can become remarkably refined. Even without

explicit training, individuals (or animals) can develop highly sensitive pattern recognition.

4. Even untrained observers (like Hans) can develop sophisticated pattern recognition.

5. Our intuitive understanding often precedes our conscious awareness as the ability to pick up on nonverbal cues happens instinctively before conscious realization.

The Clever Hans phenomenon serves as a bridge to understanding intuition—our brain's ability to process subtle cues and information below the threshold of conscious awareness. Just as Hans developed an intuitive understanding of human behavior patterns, we too can train ourselves to better recognize and interpret the subtle signals that others constantly send through their nonverbal communication.

APPLICATION OF OBSERVATION SKILLS IN VARIOUS FIELDS

Observation skills are versatile and essential across disciplines, enhancing accuracy and insight from scientific research to interpersonal relationships (Benson & Kirby, 2019). Whether in science, art, investigation, or social contexts, these skills offer powerful ways to capture and interpret information in unique ways:

Scientific Observation

In science, observation forms the basis of empirical research and helps uncover natural patterns. For instance, field scientists studying wildlife rely on meticulous observation to track animal behaviors and interactions, which provides valuable data for ecological research (Porges, 2007). Detailed notetaking and instruments like microscopes or spectrometers reduce subjective bias, allowing researchers to verify findings across repeated trials (Duchowski, 2007). These rigorous methods strengthen scientific conclusions and create reliable frameworks for future studies.

Artistic Observation

Artists rely on observation to capture the essence and emotional quality of their subjects. A landscape artist, for example, may carefully observe light, shadow, and color variations throughout the day to convey a specific mood or time (Gilchrist, 2011). Similarly, portrait artists closely study facial features and expressions to reveal the personality or emotional state of their subjects (Ekman, 2009). In digital art, animators observe real-life movements and details to recreate natural motions, bringing characters to life with an authenticity that resonates with audiences (Mehrabian, 1972).

Investigative Observation

Observation is a cornerstone of investigative fields, where attention to detail can make or break a case. Detectives, for instance, may observe suspects for inconsistencies in body language or facial expressions that suggest deception. Journalists conducting investigative work often look for incongruities in documents or interview responses, which can lead to groundbreaking revelations. In cybersecurity, analysts observe patterns in network activity to detect anomalies that could indicate security breaches or fraud, helping prevent potential threats (DePaulo *et al.*, 2003; Honts *et al.*, 2009).

Social Observation and Emotional Intelligence

In social settings, observation skills enhance emotional intelligence, helping individuals navigate complex interpersonal dynamics. For example, in a corporate meeting, a manager might observe employees' body language and facial expressions to gauge engagement or tension. In counseling or therapy, practitioners rely on observing subtle cues, like shifts in tone or micro-expressions, to understand their clients' underlying emotions. Similarly, teachers observe students' nonverbal cues to assess comprehension or emotional well-being, enabling them to adjust their approach for better engagement and support (Hall *et al.*, 2005; Mehrabian, 1971).

Challenge Yourself with 'Observation Exercises and Games'

The "One New Thing" Daily Challenge: Each day, challenge yourself to notice one new thing in your regular environment. This could be a detail in your home, on your commute, or at your workplace.

People-Watching Exercises

- In a public place, choose a person to observe for five minutes. Note their appearance, behavior, and interactions.
- Try to infer information about people based on observable details (*e.g.*, profession, mood, relationships with others present).

Nature Observation Activities

- Keep a nature journal, recording daily observations about weather, plants, and animals.
- Practice identifying bird species by sight and sound.
- Observe and sketch the same natural scene at different times of day or in different seasons.

Observation Games

- ***"I Spy":*** Play this classic game to sharpen visual observation skills.
- ***"What's Missing?":*** Arrange a group of objects, allow someone to observe them, then remove one and see if they can identify what's missing.
- ***"Spot the Difference":*** Compare two similar images to find subtle differences.

Observation Ethics and Privacy Considerations

As you develop your observation skills, it is crucial to consider ethical implications:

- ***Respect Others' Privacy:*** Avoid intrusive observation or recording without consent.
- ***Be Aware of Legal Boundaries:*** Understand laws regarding surveillance and privacy in public spaces.
- ***Use Discretion:*** Consider the potential impact of sharing your observations, especially regarding other people.
- ***Practice Cultural Sensitivity:*** Be aware that norms around observation and privacy may vary in different cultural contexts.

CONCLUSION

Mastering the art of observation can transform your experience of the world, leading to greater understanding, creativity, and connection with your environment. By engaging in all your senses, practicing mindfulness, overcoming biases, and regularly challenging your observational abilities, you can develop a heightened awareness that enriches both your personal and professional life. Remember, everyone has the capacity to become a skilled observer. It is not about having superhuman senses but about learning to pay attention in new and more effective ways. As you continue to practice and refine your observation skills, you'll likely find that the world becomes a richer, more fascinating place—full of details, patterns, and wonders that you might have previously overlooked.

Class Activity: "Detail Detective"

The "Detail Detective" activity is designed to sharpen participants' observation skills by challenging them to recall details from a complex image after a brief exposure. This exercise helps illustrate the importance of attention to detail and fosters strategies for improving memory retention, which are valuable in professions requiring keen observation.

Duration: 30 minutes

Materials needed: Complex image (*e.g.*, busy street scene), timer, notepads, pens

Instructions:

1. Show participants a complex image for 30 seconds, then remove it.
2. Give 2 minutes for participants to write down as many details as they can remember.
3. Show the image again, allowing participants to check their observations.
4. Discuss strategies for improving observation:
   - How can we train ourselves to notice more details quickly?
   - What techniques can help in remembering observed details?
   - How might enhanced observation skills benefit various professions?

CHAPTER 10

Beyond the Five Senses: Exploring Intuition and Beyond-Sense Awareness

Abstract: Intuition, often described as a "gut feeling" or "sixth sense," plays a significant role in human decision-making, yet its mechanisms remain mysterious. This chapter delves into the science and psychology behind intuition, exploring how our subconscious mind processes subtle nonverbal cues to guide instinctive reactions. It discusses the concept of hidden perception, examining theories that explain our intuitive abilities and the idea of an expanded awareness beyond the five senses. This chapter examines research into remote viewing and telepathy, highlighting challenges in scientific validation. Practical techniques for developing intuition, including mindfulness and emotional sensitivity, are provided to help readers refine their instincts. Furthermore, the chapter offers guidance on distinguishing between genuine intuitive insights and cognitive biases that can lead to erroneous conclusions. By blending scientific inquiry with openness to new possibilities, the chapter invites readers to explore the mysteries of intuition and its potential to enhance decision-making and awareness.

Keywords: Cognitive biases, Gut feeling, Hidden perception, Intuition, Subconscious mind.

INTRODUCTION

While the five traditional senses form the foundation of our perceptual experience, many people report experiences that seem to transcend these conventional modes of observation. This chapter explores the intriguing world of what is often called the "sixth sense" or even "seventh sense," encompassing phenomena such as intuition, gut feelings, and various forms of hidden perception. While these concepts remain controversial in scientific circles, their prevalence in human experience and potential impact on decision-making and interpersonal interactions make them worthy of exploration in the context of advanced observation skills (Lieberman, 2000).

Understanding the Concept of Intuition

Intuition is often described as a "gut feeling" or the ability to make decisions or understand things without the need for deliberate, conscious thought. It is an automatic, almost instantaneous understanding or perception of something, often without clear evidence or reasoning. The case of Clever Hans exemplifies how intuition can arise from subtle, nonverbal cues processed subconsciously (Pfungst, 1911). It can be better understood as a subconscious process that draws on past experiences, accumulated knowledge, and emotional insights. Rather than being a random or unfounded feeling, intuition is shaped by our brain's ability to process vast amounts of information quickly, often based on patterns or experiences we might not even be consciously aware of. For example, a seasoned detective might instantly sense when something does not feel right in an investigation, not because they have direct evidence but because their brain is subconsciously noticing inconsistencies or familiar patterns.

In essence, intuition operates on the principle of rapid pattern recognition—where the brain connects dots that might take conscious thought too long to process. It's closely tied to both emotional responses and prior learning, explaining why people often "just know" things, even if they cannot explain how or why. It blends cognitive processes with emotional intelligence and can be an essential tool in decision-making, especially in situations where time is limited or data is incomplete. Key aspects of intuition include (Lieberman, 2000; Proske & Gandevia, 2012):

Rapid Processing

Intuitive responses often arise almost instantly, bypassing the slower, deliberate process of logical reasoning. In urgent situations, intuition allows for quick decisions by relying on accumulated experiences and patterns rather than laborious analysis. Unlike deliberate thought, intuition feels like it "just happens," often giving the sensation of a spontaneous realization.

Emotional Cues in Intuition

Intuitive insights are often accompanied by a physical or emotional sensation, like a sense of comfort, unease, or excitement. According to neuroscientist Antonio Damasio, bodily responses, or "somatic markers," contribute to decision-making. These emotional cues help us weigh options based on subtle physical signals, even if we're not fully aware of them. People with high emotional intelligence may have more refined intuitive responses as they are better attuned to their feelings and the emotions of others.

Unconscious Pattern Recognition

The brain stores countless experiences, which, though often unnoticed, create patterns we can draw upon unconsciously. Developed by psychologist Gary

Klein, this model suggests that people use intuition to identify familiar patterns in situations, leading to quick and effective decisions. Intuition operates through mental shortcuts, allowing people to identify potential solutions based on cues rather than detailed analysis.

Intuition in Everyday Life

- *Protective Instincts*: Sensing potential danger—like a sudden discomfort about a person or place—may lead to avoiding it, often with good reason.
- *Problem-Solving*: Solutions to complex problems sometimes "come to mind" without conscious reasoning, as the mind unconsciously synthesizes relevant experiences and knowledge.
- *Empathy and Social Perception*: Sometimes, we can sense someone's mood or intentions without obvious cues. This intuition in social contexts often emerges from subtle behavioral signals processed unconsciously.

WHAT DO WE UNDERSTAND BY HIDDEN SENSES?

Human perception is traditionally limited to five senses. These senses allow us to interact with the world around us and form the foundation of our experience. However, over time, scholars, philosophers, and spiritual practitioners have speculated about additional forms of perception—senses that transcend the basic five and offer deeper insights into our consciousness, emotions, and even the universe itself. Beyond the traditional senses lies a realm of "extra" perceptive abilities, often referred to as intuitive, spiritual, or heightened senses. These expanded senses invite us to consider new ways of understanding the world and ourselves. They reflect the complexity of the human mind and body, as well as the depth of our potential to perceive reality in ways that go beyond mere physical stimuli. We further explore senses such as the 6th **sense** of intuition, the 7th **sense** of proprioception (body awareness), the 8th **sense** of interoception (internal body awareness), and more metaphysical concepts like the 9th **sense** of collective consciousness, the 10th **sense** of cosmic awareness, and the 11th **sense** of divine insight. Each of these "senses" represents a different facet of human perception that connects us to deeper levels of awareness, emotions, and even the universe (Hall, 1966; Hess, 1975).

6th Sense – Intuition

6th Sense is the ability to understand or know something without the need for conscious reasoning. It is the brain's way of processing subtle cues and information that we may not be consciously aware of. Its main characteristics are to be quick, instinctive understanding or insight that does not require logical reasoning. It often guides decisions and judgments (Lieberman, 2000). *For example,* to feel that something is right or wrong without knowing why or deciding quickly without needing all the details.

7th Sense – Proprioception

Proprioception is the sense that allows us to perceive the position, movement, and orientation of our body parts in space, even without looking at them. Its main characteristics involve awareness of our limbs' movements, posture, and balance. It is responsible for coordinated movement and spatial awareness (Proske & Gandevia, 2012). For *example, knowing* where your hand is when you close your eyes or walk without watching your feet.

8th Sense – Interoception

Interoception refers to the ability to sense internal bodily states such as hunger, thirst, heart rate, and breathing. It allows us to feel what is happening inside our body. It involves the characteristics of awareness of internal cues like discomfort, stress, or relaxation, which is vital for emotional regulation and health (Critchley & Gaarfinkel, 2017). *For example,* feeling thirsty, recognizing when you need to breathe deeply, or sensing your heartbeat when stressed.

CONTROVERSY SURROUNDING HIDDEN PERCEPTION

Hidden Perception, sometimes called the seventh sense, refers to the alleged ability to acquire information through means other than the known physical senses. Common types of claimed perception include Hidden Perception, or the "seventh sense," which is a controversial topic, often met with skepticism due to a lack of scientific validation. Hidden Perception encompasses various phenomena where information seems to be acquired through non-physical means beyond our five traditional senses (Hall, 1966; Hess, 1975).

Common Types of Hidden Perception

Telepathy

The purported ability to send or receive thoughts, feelings, or knowledge between individuals without any physical interaction. Experiences of knowing what someone else is thinking or feeling are often reported by people who are closely connected, such as twins or long-term partners. Critics argue that telepathy lacks reliable evidence, attributing these experiences to subconscious cues, shared experiences, or coincidence (Zahran, 2012).

Clairvoyance

A supposed ability to gain information about an object, person, or place, regardless of distance, without using conventional sensory input. Anecdotes often involve individuals describing locations or events they have no known connection to, like "seeing" an accident from afar. Many dismiss clairvoyance because of lucky guesses, imaginative interpretation, or retroactive fitting of information (Zahran, 2012).

Precognition

The alleged ability to foresee future events before they occur, sometimes experienced in the form of vivid dreams or "visions". Stories of people dreaming about major events or disasters before they happen. Skeptics attribute precognition claims to coincidence, retrospective bias (fitting vague predictions to actual events), or a misunderstanding of probability (Hess, 1975).

Why Hidden Perception Remains Controversial?

Hidden perception, often tied to subliminal messages or unconscious cognition, remains controversial due to its ambiguous evidence and interpretation. Critics argue that while some studies suggest subtle stimuli can influence behavior, the effects are inconsistent, context-dependent, and challenging to replicate (Hall, 1966; Robinson, 2009).

Challenges to Scientific Validation

- *Lack of Empirical Evidence*: Many scientists and psychologists assert that hidden perception lacks the rigorous, reproducible evidence necessary to be scientifically validated. Experiments testing hidden perception, such as those conducted by parapsychologists, often fail to produce consistent results (Zahran, 2012).
- *Skepticism from the Scientific Community*: Hidden perception challenges the current understanding of physics, biology, and psychology, as it suggests mechanisms for information transfer that are not explained by known sensory or neurological processes (Hess, 1975; Robinson, 2009).
- *Cultural and Psychological Factors*: Hidden perception is often influenced by cultural beliefs and psychological factors, which may shape people's experiences and interpretations of seemingly unexplainable events. For example, cognitive biases like confirmation bias can cause individuals to remember instances that support hidden perception's beliefs and disregard contradictory evidence (Hall, 1976).
- *Cognitive and Perceptual Biases*: Studies have shown that the human mind is

predisposed to seek patterns and ascribe meaning to random events, leading to the interpretation of coincidences as " Hidden Perception " insights (Langer, 1989).

Arguments in Support of Hidden Perception

- *Parapsychology Research*: Parapsychologists have conducted experiments, such as the Ganzfeld experiment, aiming to detect weak hidden perception signals. While results have been inconclusive, advocates argue that certain findings merit further investigation (Zahran, 2012).
- *Quantum Theory Speculation*: Some advocates draw parallels to quantum theory, suggesting that phenomena like entanglement hint at non-local connections that might, theoretically, allow for hidden perception. However, this remains speculative and unsupported by direct evidence (Dwork & Roth, 2014).

REASONS FOR INTUITIVE AND HIDDEN OR EXTRA-SENSORY PERCEPTION-LIKE EXPERIENCES

Intuitive and hidden perception-like experiences are often compelling and can feel deeply real. While such experiences may seem to defy logical explanations, researchers have identified psychological and perceptual mechanisms that are likely to contribute to these phenomena. Here are some of the primary reasons proposed to explain why these experiences occur (Ekman, 2009; Hall, 1966; Hess, 1975; Lieberman, 2000; Zahran, 2012):

Subconscious Observation

Our brains are highly attuned to subtle environmental cues, which are often processed below the level of conscious awareness. This can lead to insights or "gut feelings" that feel intuitive. In social settings, subtle cues like changes in body language, vocal tone, or facial expressions may be picked up by our subconscious, leading to an accurate "intuition" about someone's mood or intentions. Although we aren't consciously aware of noticing these cues, our brain integrates them to create a holistic impression, which can feel like an intuitive or hidden perception experience.

Probability and Coincidence

With enough daily interactions and events, coincidences are statistically inevitable. However, our minds are wired to seek meaning, so we tend to notice and remember coincidences that feel significant. Having a premonition about a friend calling and then receiving their call shortly after may feel like a hidden perception, but it is often just an instance of probability aligning with a memorable outcome. Many seemingly "extraordinary" experiences can be attributed to random chance. We remember the hits (when a hunch proves correct) and often ignore or forget the misses (when it does not), creating the impression of something paranormal.

Cold Reading Techniques

Cold reading is a skill that involves making educated guesses about a person based on subtle cues, body language, and general knowledge of human behavior. This technique is often used by performers and can create the illusion of psychic abilities. A psychic might make general statements that apply to many people or use non-verbal cues to "read" the client's reactions and adjust their statements accordingly. Cold reading relies on the brain's ability to interpret feedback and refine guesses in real time.

Selective Memory and Confirmation Bias

Confirmation bias is the tendency to seek, interpret, and remember information that supports our existing beliefs while ignoring or discounting information that contradicts them. If someone believes they have a gift for predicting the future, they may vividly recall the times their predictions were accurate while forgetting or minimizing occasions when they were wrong. Selective memory and confirmation bias reinforce the belief in intuition by creating a mental record that seems supportive, even if it is not reflective of reality. This selective focus shapes our perceptions of frequency and accuracy, reinforcing belief in hidden perceptions.

To fully harness both intuitive and analytical approaches to observation, balanced and mindful practice is essential. Here is how to make the most of these complementary skills:

Practice Active Observation

Deliberately tune into your surroundings using all sensory inputs—sight, sound, touch, taste, and smell—rather than relying solely on one sense. Move beyond mere noticing; actively describe what you're observing to create a detailed mental record, enhancing memory and awareness for intuitive insights.

Combine Intuition with Analysis

Treat intuitive insights as hypotheses to explore further rather than immediate conclusions. This encourages a systematic approach to validate or refine initial impressions. After observing something intuitively, apply analytical methods to look for patterns, anomalies, or specific details that support or challenge your impression.

Develop a Personal Framework

Recognize different forms of intuition (*e.g.*, gut feelings about people, situational awareness, pattern recognition). Categorizing these types can help track patterns in your intuitive successes. Over time, note the consistency of each intuition type's accuracy, building a clearer picture of when and where your intuitive responses tend to be most reliable.

Seek Feedback

Regularly compare your intuitive impressions with objective outcomes to refine and calibrate your observation skills. Accept that intuition can be imperfect. Continuously seeking feedback from trusted sources or objective data can enhance your skills and reduce potential biases.

By combining these practices, you can cultivate a well-rounded observational approach that incorporates the insights of intuition with the rigor of analysis. This balanced method enhances accuracy, deepens understanding, and ultimately improves decision-making in diverse contexts.

CONCLUSION

The fields of intuition and hidden perception continue to captivate both scientific and philosophical inquiry. While the scientific validation of phenomena like intuitive abilities remains uncertain, there is value in recognizing the role of intuition in our personal decision-making processes. By cultivating a balanced and open-minded approach, we can explore intuition as a tool that complements traditional observation skills, enhancing both our perception and judgment. Developing intuitive capabilities, whether seen as a literal sixth sense or as a product of subconscious processing, can broaden our awareness and improve decision-making. As with all skills, it is through consistent practice, introspection, and an openness to new ideas that we can refine and expand our perceptual toolkit.

Class Activity: "Intuition Experiment"

The "Intuition Experiment" activity encourages participants to explore their intuitive abilities by guessing which hand holds a hidden object based on subtle impressions. After multiple rounds, participants record their success rates and reflect on their intuitive experiences. The activity sparks discussion on the role of intuition in decision-making and how it can complement observable nonverbal cues in real-world situations.

Duration: 40 minutes

Materials needed: Small objects (*e.g.*, coins), notepads, pens

Instructions:

1. Pair up participants.
2. One person hides a small object in one hand behind their back.
3. The other person tries to intuit which hand holds the object, noting any feelings or impressions.
4. Repeat 10 times, then switch roles.
5. Participants record their success rate and any patterns they noticed.
6. Discuss as a group:
   - Did anyone perform significantly above chance?
   - What sensations or impressions did people experience when trying to use intuition?
   - How might intuition complement more observable nonverbal cues in real-world scenarios?

REFERENCES

Adolphs, R. (2002). Neural systems for recognizing emotion. *Curr. Opin. Neurobiol, 12*(2), 169-177.
[http://dx.doi.org/10.1016/S0959-4388(02)00301-X] [PMID: 12015233]

Allen, M. (2021). The ethics of observation: Balancing research and privacy. *J. Soc. Sci, 45*(3), 267-280.

Ambady, N., Weisbuch, M. (2010). Nonverbal behavior. In: Fiske, S.T., Gilbert, D.T., Lindzey, G., (Eds.), *Handbook of social psychology*. John Wiley & Sons. 464-497..
[http://dx.doi.org/10.1002/9780470561119.socpsy001013]

Ambady, N., LaPlante, D., Nguyen, T. (2002). The mind in the eyes: Evidence for the role of emotion recognition in empathy. *J. Pers. Soc. Psychol, 81*(6), 1109-1124.
[http://dx.doi.org/10.1037/0022-3514.81.6.1109]

Amsel, T.T. (2019). An urban legend called: "The 7/38/55 ratio rule.". *European Polygraph, 13*(2), 95-99.
[http://dx.doi.org/10.2478/ep-2019-0007]

Andersen, P.A. (2008). *Nonverbal communication: Forms and functions* Waveland Press.

Argyle, M. (1988). *Bodily communication* Routledge.
[http://dx.doi.org/10.4324/9780203753835]

Argyle, M., Cook, M. (1976). *Gaze and mutual gaze*. Cambridge University Press.

Argyle, M., Dean, J. (1965). Eye-contact, distance and affiliation. *Sociometry, 28*(3), 289-304.
[http://dx.doi.org/10.2307/2786027] [PMID: 14341239]

Axtell, R.E. (1998). *Gestures: The do's and taboos of body language around the world*. John Wiley & Sons.

Bailey, B.P., Konstan, J.A. (2006). On the need for attention-aware systems: Measuring effects of interruption on task performance, error rate, and affective state. *Comput. Human Behav, 22*(4), 685-708.
[http://dx.doi.org/10.1016/j.chb.2005.12.009]

Burgoon, J.K., Guerrero, L.K., Floyd, K. (2016). *Nonverbal Communication*. Routledge.
[http://dx.doi.org/10.4324/9781315663425]

Benson, P., Kirby, S. (2019). Privacy in the digital age: Implications for observational research. *Ethics Behav, 29*(5), 382-396.

Birdwhistell, R.L. (1952). *Introduction to kinesics: An annotation system for analysis of body motion and gesture*. University of Louisville.

Birdwhistell, R.L. (1970). *Kinesics and context: Essays on body motion communication*. University of Pennsylvania Press.

Bissinger, B., Beer, A., Märtin, C., Fellmann, M. (2023). Emotion recognition *via* facial expressions to improve virtual communication in videoconferences. In: Kurosu, M., Hashizume, A., (Eds.), *Human-Computer Interaction. HCII 2023* Lecture Notes in Computer ScienceSpringer.
[http://dx.doi.org/10.1007/978-3-031-35599-8_10]

Bond, C.F., Jr, DePaulo, B.M. (2006). Accuracy of deception judgments. *Pers. Soc. Psychol. Rev, 10*(3),

214-234.
[http://dx.doi.org/10.1207/s15327957pspr1003_2] [PMID: 16859438]

Bradley, M.M., Miccoli, L., Escrig, M.A., Lang, P.J. (2008). The pupil as a measure of emotional arousal and autonomic activation. *Psychophysiology, 45*(4), 602-607.
[http://dx.doi.org/10.1111/j.1469-8986.2008.00654.x] [PMID: 18282202]

Burgoon, J.K., Guerrero, L.K., Floyd, K. (2016). *Nonverbal communication.* Routledge.
[http://dx.doi.org/10.4324/9781315663425]

Carney, D.R., Cuddy, A.J.C., Yap, A.J. (2010). Power Posing. *Psychol. Sci, 21*(10), 1363-1368.
[http://dx.doi.org/10.1177/0956797610383437] [PMID: 20855902]

Chen, L. (2022). Cultural perspectives on privacy and observation. *International Journal of Cross-Cultural Studies, 17*(2), 103-118.

Cheung, W.J., Patey, A.M., Frank, J.R., Mackay, M., Boet, S. (2019). Barriers and enablers to direct observation of trainees' clinical performance: A qualitative study using the theoretical domains framework. *Acad. Med, 94*(1), 101-114.
[http://dx.doi.org/10.1097/ACM.0000000000002396] [PMID: 30095454]

Critchley, H.D. (2005). Neural mechanisms of autonomic, affective, and cognitive integration. *J. Comp. Neurol, 493*(1), 154-166.
[http://dx.doi.org/10.1002/cne.20749] [PMID: 16254997]

Critchley, H.D., Garfinkel, S.N. (2017). Interoception and emotion. *Curr. Opin. Psychol, 17*, 7-14.
[http://dx.doi.org/10.1016/j.copsyc.2017.04.020] [PMID: 28950976]

Darwin, C. (1872). *The expression of the emotions in man and animals.* John Murray.
[http://dx.doi.org/10.1037/10001-000]

Dael, N., Mortillaro, M., Scherer, K.R. (2012). Emotion expression in body action and posture. *Emotion, 12*(5), 1085-1101.
[http://dx.doi.org/10.1037/a0025737] [PMID: 22059517]

DePaulo, B.M., Lindsay, J.J., Malone, B.E., Muhlenbruck, L., Charlton, K., Cooper, H. (2003). Cues to deception. *Psychol. Bull, 129*(1), 74-118.
[http://dx.doi.org/10.1037/0033-2909.129.1.74] [PMID: 12555795]

Duchowski, A.T. (2007). *Eye tracking methodology: Theory and practice* Springer-Verlag.

Duncan, S. (1972). Some signals and rules for taking speaking turns in conversations. *J. Pers. Soc. Psychol, 23*(2), 283-292.
[http://dx.doi.org/10.1037/h0033031]

Dwork, C., Roth, A. (2013). The algorithmic foundations of differential privacy. *Foundations and Trends® in Theoretical Computer Science, 9*(3-4), 211-407.
[http://dx.doi.org/10.1561/0400000042]

Egan, G. (2013). *The skilled helper: A problem-management and opportunity-development approach to helping* Cengage Learning.

Eicher, J.B., Ross, D.H. (2010). *Berg encyclopedia of world dress and fashion* Berg Publishers.
[http://dx.doi.org/10.2752/BEWDF/EDv10]

Ekman, P. (1972). *Emotion in the human face.* Pergamon Press.

Ekman, P. (1993). Facial expression and emotion. *Am. Psychol, 48*(4), 384-392.
[http://dx.doi.org/10.1037/0003-066X.48.4.384] [PMID: 8512154]

Ekman, P. (2003). *Emotions revealed: Recognizing faces and feelings to improve communication and emotional life.* Times Books.

Ekman, P. (2009). *Telling lies: Clues to deceit in the marketplace, politics, and marriage* W.W. Norton & Company.

Ekman, P., Friesen, W. (1969). The repertoire of nonverbal behavior: Categories, origins, usage, and coding. *Semiotica, 1*(1), 49-98.
[http://dx.doi.org/10.1515/semi.1969.1.1.49]

Ekman, P., Friesen, W.V. (1971). Constants across cultures in the face and emotion. *J. Pers. Soc. Psychol, 17*(2), 124-129.
[http://dx.doi.org/10.1037/h0030377] [PMID: 5542557]

Ekman, P., Friesen, W.V. (1975). *Unmasking the face: A guide to recognizing emotions from facial clues.* Malor Books.

European Union. (2018). General Data Protection Regulation (GDPR). *Official Journal of the European Union, L 119/1.*

Frischen, A., Bayliss, A.P., Tipper, S.P. (2007). Gaze cueing of attention: Visual attention, social cognition, and individual differences. *Psychol. Bull, 133*(4), 694-724.
[http://dx.doi.org/10.1037/0033-2909.133.4.694] [PMID: 17592962]

Gallese, V., Keysers, C., Rizzolatti, G. (2004). A unifying view of the basis of social cognition. *Trends Cogn. Sci, 8*(9), 396-403.
[http://dx.doi.org/10.1016/j.tics.2004.07.002] [PMID: 15350240]

Gilchrist, I.D. (2011). Saccades. In: Liversedge, S.P., Gilchrist, I.D., Everling, S., (Eds.), *The Oxford Handbook of Eye Movements* Oxford University Press.

Goberman, A.M., Coelho, C. (2002). Acoustic analysis of Parkinsonian speech I: Speech characteristics and L-Dopa therapy. *NeuroRehabilitation, 17*(3), 237-246.
[http://dx.doi.org/10.3233/NRE-2002-17310] [PMID: 12237505]

Goman, C.K. (2011). *The silent language of leaders: How body language can help—or hurt—how you lead.* Jossey-Bass.

Graziano, M.S.A. (2022). The origin of smiling, laughing, and crying: The defensive mimic theory. *Evol. Hum. Sci, 4*, e10.
[http://dx.doi.org/10.1017/ehs.2022.5] [PMID: 37588928]

Gross, J.J. (2002). Emotion regulation: Affective, cognitive, and social consequences. *Psychophysiology, 39*(3), 281-291.
[http://dx.doi.org/10.1017/S0048577201393198] [PMID: 12212647]

Gross, J.J., John, O.P. (1995). Facets of emotional Expressivity: Three self-report factors and their correlates. *Pers. Individ. Dif, 19*(4), 555-568.

[http://dx.doi.org/10.1016/0191-8869(95)00055-B]

Gunawan, A.B., Pratama, B., Sarwono, R. (2021). Digital proxemics approach in cyber space analysis – A systematic literature review. *ICIC Express Lett, 15*(2), 201-208.
[http://dx.doi.org/10.24507/icicel.15.02.201]

Hall, E.T. (1966). *The hidden dimension.* Doubleday.

Hall, E.T. (1976). *Beyond culture.* Anchor Books.

Hall, J.A., Coats, E.J., LeBeau, L.S. (2005). Nonverbal behavior and the vertical dimension of social relations: a meta-analysis. *Psychol. Bull, 131*(6), 898-924.
[http://dx.doi.org/10.1037/0033-2909.131.6.898] [PMID: 16351328]

Hall, J.A., Harrigan, J.A., Rosenthal, R. (1995). Nonverbal behavior in clinician—patient interaction. *Appl. Prev. Psychol, 4*(1), 21-37.
[http://dx.doi.org/10.1016/S0962-1849(05)80049-6]

Hall, J.A., Horgan, T.G., Murphy, N.A. (2019). Nonverbal communication and counseling outcome. *Couns. Psychol. Q, 32*(4), 476-492.
[http://dx.doi.org/10.1080/09515070.2019.1585540]

Hansraj, K.K. (2014). Assessment of stresses in the cervical spine caused by posture and position of the head. *Surg. Technol. Int, 25*, 277-279.
[PMID: 25393825]

Harrigan, J.A., Rosenthal, R., Scherer, K.R. (2005). *The new handbook of methods in nonverbal behavior research.* Oxford University Press.
[http://dx.doi.org/10.1093/oso/9780198529613.001.0001]

Hatfield, E., Cacioppo, J.T., Rapson, R.L. (1994). *Emotional Contagion.* Cambridge University Press.

Heiting, G. (2019). *What causes dilated pupils?.* All About Vision. Available https://www.allaboutvision.com/conditions/dilated-pupils.htm

Heller, E. (2009). *Psychologie de la couleur: effets et symboliques.* Pyramid.

Henderson, J. (2003). Human gaze control during real-world scene perception. *Trends Cogn. Sci, 7*(11), 498-504.
[http://dx.doi.org/10.1016/j.tics.2003.09.006] [PMID: 14585447]

Herring, S.C., Dainas, A.R. (2018). Receiver interpretations of emoji functions: A gender perspective. In: Wijeratne, S., Kiciman, E., Saggion, H., Sheth, A., (Eds.), *Proceedings of the 1st International Workshop on Emoji Understanding and Applications in Social Media (Emoji2018).* Stanford, CA, USA: CEUR Workshop Proceedings. Available http://ceur-ws.org

Hess, E.H. (1975). *The tell-tale eye: How your eyes reveal hidden thoughts and emotions.* Van Nostrand Reinhold.

Hess, U., Adams, R.B., Jr, Kleck, R.E. (2009). The face is not an empty canvas: how facial expressions interact with facial appearance. *Philos. Trans. R. Soc. Lond. B Biol. Sci, 364*(1535), 3497-3504.
[http://dx.doi.org/10.1098/rstb.2009.0165] [PMID: 19884144]

Higbee, K.L. (2001). *Your Memory: How It Works and How to Improve It.* (Illustrated, Revised ed.). Marlowe & Company.

Honts, C. R., Hartwig, M., Kleinman, S. M., Meissner, C. A. (2009). Credibility assessment at portals of entry: Portals of entry and the detection of deception. *Final report to CIFA DOD.*

Howlett, N., Pine, K.J., Cahill, N., Orakçıoğlu, İ., Fletcher, B. (2015). Unbuttoned: The interaction between provocativeness of female work attire and occupational status. *Sex Roles, 72*(3-4), 105-116. [http://dx.doi.org/10.1007/s11199-015-0450-8]

Huttner, J-P., Robra-Bissantz, S. (2017). An immersive memory palace: Supporting the method of loci with virtual reality. *Proceedings of the Twenty-Third Americas Conference on Information Systems,* 1-10.

Ioannou, S., Gallese, V., Merla, A. (2014). Thermal infrared imaging in psychophysiology: Potentialities and limits. *Psychophysiology, 51*(10), 951-963. [http://dx.doi.org/10.1111/psyp.12243] [PMID: 24961292]

JavaTpoint. (2024). *Advantages and disadvantages of non-verbal communication.* Available https://www.javatpoint.com/advantages-and-disadvantages-of-non-verbal-communication

Johnson, R. (2020). Ethical considerations in ethnographic research. *Qualitative Research Methods, 12*(4), 289-304.

Jourard, S.M. (1966). An exploratory study of body-accessibility. *Br. J. Soc. Clin. Psychol, 5*(3), 221-231. [http://dx.doi.org/10.1111/j.2044-8260.1966.tb00978.x] [PMID: 5975653]

Kahneman, D., Beatty, J. (1966). Pupil diameter and load on memory. *Science, 154*(3756), 1583-1585. [http://dx.doi.org/10.1126/science.154.3756.1583] [PMID: 5924930]

Kavanagh, E., Kimock, C., Whitehouse, J., Micheletta, J., Waller, B.M. (2022). Revisiting Darwin's comparisons between human and non-human primate facial signals. *Evol. Hum. Sci, 4*, e27. [http://dx.doi.org/10.1017/ehs.2022.26] [PMID: 35821665]

Keltner, D. (1995). Signs of appeasement: Evidence for the distinct displays of embarrassment, amusement, and shame. *J. Pers. Soc. Psychol, 68*(3), 441-454. [http://dx.doi.org/10.1037/0022-3514.68.3.441]

Kendon, A. (2004). *Gesture: Visible Action as Utterance.* Cambridge University Press. [http://dx.doi.org/10.1017/CBO9780511807572]

Kleinke, C.L. (1986). Gaze and eye contact: A research review. *Psychol. Bull, 100*(1), 78-100. [http://dx.doi.org/10.1037/0033-2909.100.1.78] [PMID: 3526377]

Knapp, M.L., Hall, J.A., Horgan, T.G. (2013). *Nonverbal communication in human interaction* Wadsworth.

Kring, A.M., Gordon, A.H. (1998). Sex differences in emotion: Expression, experience, and physiology. *J. Pers. Soc. Psychol, 74*(3), 686-703. [http://dx.doi.org/10.1037/0022-3514.74.3.686] [PMID: 9523412]

Lakin, J.L. (2006). Automatic cognitive processes and nonverbal communication. In: Manusov, V., Patterson, M.L., (Eds.), *The SAGE handbook of nonverbal communication* SAGE Publications. [http://dx.doi.org/10.4135/9781412976152.n4]

Langer, E. J. (1989). *Mindfulness.* Addison-Wesley/Addison Wesley Longman.

Lazarus, R.S. (1991). *Emotion and adaptation.* Oxford University Press.

[http://dx.doi.org/10.1093/oso/9780195069945.001.0001]

Lieberman, M.D. (2000). Intuition: A social cognitive neuroscience approach. *Psychol. Bull,* *126*(1), 109-137.
[http://dx.doi.org/10.1037/0033-2909.126.1.109] [PMID: 10668352]

Levine, T.R. (2014). Truth-Default Theory (TDT). *J. Lang. Soc. Psychol,* *33*(4), 378-392.
[http://dx.doi.org/10.1177/0261927X14535916]

Media, H. (2024). *Colour psychology in branding.* The Halo Media Group. Available https://www.halo-media.com/colour-psychology-in-branding/

Manusov, V., Patterson, M.L. (2006). *The SAGE handbook of nonverbal communication.* SAGE Publications.
[http://dx.doi.org/10.4135/9781412976152]

Maroni, B., Gnisci, A., Pontecorvo, C. (2008). Turn-taking in classroom interactions. *J. Pragmatics,* *40*(6), 1060-1084.
[http://dx.doi.org/10.1016/j.pragma.2008.01.007]

Mathôt, S. (2018). Pupillometry: Psychology, physiology, and function. *Journal of Cognition,* *1*(1), 16, 1–23.
[http://dx.doi.org/10.5334/joc.18]

Matsumoto, D., Hwang, H.S. (2013). *Nonverbal communication: Science and applications.* SAGE Publications.
[http://dx.doi.org/10.4135/9781452244037]

Mehrabian, A. (1971). *Silent messages* Wadsworth.

Mehrabian, A. (1972). *Nonverbal Communication* Routledge.
[http://dx.doi.org/10.4324/9781351308724]

Mehu, M., Scherer, K.R. (2012). A psycho-ethological approach to social signal processing. *Cogn. Process,* *13*(S2) (Suppl. 2), 397-414.
[http://dx.doi.org/10.1007/s10339-012-0435-2] [PMID: 22328016]

Michalak, J., Mischnat, J., Teismann, T. (2014). Sitting posture makes a difference-embodiment effects on depressive memory bias. *Clin. Psychol. Psychother,* *21*(6), 519-524.
[http://dx.doi.org/10.1002/cpp.1890] [PMID: 24577937]

Miyake, N., Norman, D.A. (1979). To ask a question, one must know enough to know what is not known. *J. Verbal Learn. Verbal Behav,* *18*(3), 357-364.
[http://dx.doi.org/10.1016/S0022-5371(79)90200-7]

Morris, D., Collett, P., Marsh, P., O'Shaughnessy, M. (2002). *Gestures: Their origins and distribution.* Scarborough House.

Noroozi, F., Corneanu, C.A., Kamińska, D., Sapiński, T., Escalera, S., Anbarjafari, G. (2021). Survey on emotional body gesture recognition. *IEEE Trans. Affect. Comput,* *12*(2), 505-523.
[http://dx.doi.org/10.1109/TAFFC.2018.2874986]

Oggiano, M. (2023). Ocular behavior. *Misunderstandings about non-verbal communication* Springer.
[http://dx.doi.org/10.1007/978-3-031-43571-3_3]

Patterson, M.L. (2001). *The evolution of nonverbal communication: The influence of culture on interpersonal behavior.* MIT Press.

Pfungst, O. (1911). *Clever Hans (the Horse of Mr. von Osten): A Contribution to Experimental Animal and Human Psychology.* New York: Henry Holt and Compan.
[http://dx.doi.org/10.5962/bhl.title.56164]

Patterson, M.L. (2011). *Nonverbal behavior: Psychology of face-to-face communication.* Routledge.

Pease, A., Pease, B. (2004). *The Definitive Book of Body Language.* Australia: Pease International.

Pease, A., Pease, B. (2017). *The definitive book of body language: How to read others' attitudes by their gestures.* Orion.

Porges, S.W. (2007). The polyvagal perspective. *Biol. Psychol, 74*(2), 116-143.
[http://dx.doi.org/10.1016/j.biopsycho.2006.06.009] [PMID: 17049418]

Proske, U., Gandevia, S.C. (2012). The proprioceptive senses: their roles in signaling body shape, body position and movement, and muscle force. *Physiol. Rev, 92*(4), 1651-1697.
[http://dx.doi.org/10.1152/physrev.00048.2011] [PMID: 23073629]

Rayner, K. (1998). Eye movements in reading and information processing: 20 years of research. *Psychol. Bull, 124*(3), 372-422.
[http://dx.doi.org/10.1037/0033-2909.124.3.372] [PMID: 9849112]

Remland, M.S., Jones, T.S., Brinkman, H. (1991). Proxemic and haptic behavior in three European countries. *J. Nonverbal Behav, 15*(4), 215-232.
[http://dx.doi.org/10.1007/BF00986923]

Riggio, H.R., Riggio, R.E. (2002). Emotional expressiveness, extraversion, and neuroticism: A meta-analysis. *J. Nonverbal Behav, 26*(4), 195-218.
[http://dx.doi.org/10.1023/A:1022117500440]

Rizzolatti, G., Craighero, L. (2004). The mirror-neuron system. *Annu. Rev. Neurosci, 27*(1), 169-192.
[http://dx.doi.org/10.1146/annurev.neuro.27.070203.144230] [PMID: 15217330]

Robinson, E. (2009). Extra-sensory perception - a controversial debate. *The Psychologist.* Available https://www.bps.org.uk/psychologist/extra-sensory-perception-controversial-debate

Rout, S. (2023). *The impact of mirror neurons on our day-to-day life: Exploring the neuroscience behind empathy and social interactions*DESC World. Available https://descworld.org/the-impact-of-mirror-neu-ons-on-our-day-to-day-life-exploring-the-neuroscience-behind-empathy-and-social-interactions/

Scherer, K. (2003). Vocal communication of emotion: A review of research paradigms. *Speech Commun, 40*(1-2), 227-256.
[http://dx.doi.org/10.1016/S0167-6393(02)00084-5]

Scherer, K.R., Ellgring, H. (2007). Multimodal expression of emotion: Affect programs or componential appraisal patterns?. *Emotion, 7*(1), 158-171.
[http://dx.doi.org/10.1037/1528-3542.7.1.158] [PMID: 17352571]

Siegman, A.W., Feldstein, S. (1978). *Nonverbal behavior and communication.* Lawrence Erlbaum Associates.

Sinha, J.B.P. (2012). *Culture and Organizational Behaviour.* Sage Publication.

Sotak, K.L., Serban, A., Friedman, B.A., Palanski, M. (2024). Perceptions of ethicality: The role of attire style, attire appropriateness, and context. *J. Bus. Ethics, 189*(1), 149-175. [http://dx.doi.org/10.1007/s10551-023-05347-7] [PMID: 36818159]

Soto, C.J., John, O.P., Gosling, S.D., Potter, J. (2011). Age differences in personality traits from 10 to 65: Big Five domains and facets in a large cross-sectional sample. *J. Pers. Soc. Psychol, 100*(2), 330-348. [http://dx.doi.org/10.1037/a0021717] [PMID: 21171787]

Spector, R.H. (1990). The pupils. In: Walker, H.K., Hall, W.D., Hurst, J.W., (Eds.), *Clinical methods: The history, physical, and laboratory examinations* Butterworths. Available https://www.ncbi.nlm.nih.gov/books/NBK381/

Strack, F., Martin, L.L., Stepper, S. (1988). Inhibiting and facilitating conditions of the human smile: A nonobtrusive test of the facial feedback hypothesis. *J. Pers. Soc. Psychol, 54*(5), 768-777. [http://dx.doi.org/10.1037/0022-3514.54.5.768] [PMID: 3379579]

Sweller, J., Ayres, P., Kalyuga, S. (2011). *Cognitive Load Theory.* Springer Science & Business Media. [http://dx.doi.org/10.1007/978-1-4419-8126-4]

Tomasello, M. (2008). *Origins of human communication.* MIT Press. [http://dx.doi.org/10.7551/mitpress/7551.001.0001]

Vingerhoets, A. (2013). *Why only humans weep: Unravelling the mysteries of tears.* Oxford University Press. [http://dx.doi.org/10.1093/acprof:oso/9780198570240.001.0001]

Vrij, A. (2008). *Detecting lies and deceit: Pitfalls and opportunities* Wiley.

Vygotsky, L.S. (1987). *The collected works of L. S. Vygotsky, Volume 1: Problems of general psychology.* (R. W. Rieber & A. S. Carton, Eds.; N. Minick, Trans.). Springer. (Original work published 1934).

Watzlawick, P., Beavin, J.H., Jackson, D.D. (1967). *Pragmatics of human communication: A study of interactional patterns, pathologies, and paradoxes.* Norton.

Wu, P., Wang, W., Liu, H. (2013). Methods of recognizing true and fake smiles by using AU6 and AU12 in a holistic way. In: Sun, Z., Deng, Z., (Eds.), *Proceedings of the 2013 Chinese Intelligent Automation Conference, Vol. 25,* 65-72. [http://dx.doi.org/10.1007/978-3-642-38466-0_67]

Zahran, S.K.A.E.K. (2012). Role of the extra sensory perception in decision making and interpersonal relationships: A comparative study among pre-school children and adolescents. *Int. J. Bus. Soc. Sci, 3*(9), 91-99.

Zuckerman, M., Driver, R.E. (1985). Telling lies: Verbal and nonverbal cues. In: Berkowitz, L., (Ed.), Advances in experimental social psychologyAcademic Press.

SUBJECT INDEX

I

Impaired smooth pursuit movements 30
Impairment, cognitive 20
Implications, ethical 160
Impressions, holistic 167
Influence 119, 166
   behavior 166
   pupil dilation 119
Infrared radiation 143, 144, 145
Integrated systems 145
Interpreting 44, 120
   micro-expressions 44
   pupil dilation 120
Interrogations, police 44, 138
Interventions, enhancing mental health 115

L

Law enforcement 46, 138
   officers 46
   professionals 138
Learning disorders 31

M

Machine learning algorithms 142
Memories 71, 151, 152, 153, 155
   painful 71
Memory 147, 153, 154, 155
   palace technique 147, 153, 154, 155
   retention 155
Mental 31, 42, 104, 108, 138, 139, 155
   effort 42, 104, 139
   health conditions 108
   processes 31, 138, 155
Micro-expression(s) 22, 44, 45, 47, 143
   analysis 44, 47
   detection 22, 143
   fleeting 45
   recognition 44
Movements 29, 30, 31, 68, 70, 71, 75, 134, 137, 141, 151, 157, 165
   eyebrow 71
   natural 141
Muscles, facial 69, 102

N

Nature 7, 10, 15, 111, 112, 156, 159
   contagious 112
   multi-layered 10
   observation activities 159
Nerve damage 121
Nervous system 42, 117, 118, 131, 134
   autonomic 42, 117, 118, 134
   parasympathetic 118
Neural pathways 103
Neuroimaging 3
Neurological 121, 135, 166
   damage 121
   mechanism 135
   processes 166
Neuroticism 108
Nonverbal 16, 22, 23, 40, 73, 77, 80, 83, 85, 96, 141
   communication tools 83, 85
   cues, interpreting 22, 23, 40, 77
   expressions 16, 73, 80, 96, 141

O

Observation(s) 20, 21, 151, 152, 160
   keen 160
   naturalistic 21
   olfactory 151
   sensory 152
   systematic 20
Observation skills 148, 162, 169
   advanced 162
   developing keen 148
   traditional 169
Ocular communication 27, 117
Oxytocin, releasing 52

P

Pain, chronic 115, 135
PESTLE analysis 157
Physical 9, 56, 67, 93, 105, 151
   contact 9, 56, 67, 93, 151
   health issues 105
Pomodoro technique 149
Postural 135, 137
   analysis 135
   communication 137

www.ingramcontent.com/pod-product-compliance
Lightning Source LLC
Chambersburg PA
CBHW061135030426

42334CB00003B/42